RESPONDING TO STUDENT TRAUMA

A TOOLKIT FOR SCHOOLS IN TIMES OF CRISIS

Stephanie Filio, M.Ed.

free spirit

PUBLISHING®

Library of Congress Cataloging-in-Publication Data
This book has been filed with the Library of Congress.
LCCN: 2020943090

Free Spirit Publishing does not have control over or assume responsibility for author or third-party websites and their content. At the time of this book's publication, all facts and figures cited within are the most current available. All telephone numbers, addresses, and website URLs are accurate and active; all publications, organizations, websites, and other resources exist as described in this book; and all have been verified as of August 2020. If you find an error or believe that a resource listed here is not as described, please contact Free Spirit Publishing.

Edited by Meg Bratsch
Cover and interior design by Emily Dyer

10 9 8 7 6 5 4 3 2 1
Printed in the United States of America

Free Spirit Publishing Inc.
6325 Sandburg Road, Suite 100
Minneapolis, MN 55427-3674
(612) 338-2068
help4kids@freespirit.com
freespirit.com

FSC
www.fsc.org
MIX
Paper from
responsible sources
FSC® C005010

DEDICATION

This book is dedicated to all the students who sleep, eat, cry, write, laugh, type, read, fold paper cranes, and dare to dream in the stillness of the school counselor's office when the rest of the world is chaotic.

....

ACKNOWLEDGMENTS

I have been lucky enough to work with some of the most amazing educators in my city, state, and country. At each school I have worked in, with each administrator and every teacher relationship, I have gained more tools for my toolbox. This includes the larger educational community at Free Spirit Publishing who seek to reach students through their publishing, editing, writing, and wrangling of "free spirits" like me!

Amazing peers in our school counseling family (ayyyeeee my beautiful LKMS school counseling team!), school social workers, and the many specialists all bring another level of enrichment to our schools. They have taught me grace and teamwork and great compassion, always reminding me to remain a lifelong learner at heart. Of course, my amazing, devoted, and vocal middle school kids continue to be my central guides to better myself and my practice. They tell me what they need, and they are patient with me as I learn. They are truly our "next steps" as we navigate our developing world.

Eddie, Maddie, and Mason: thank you for always sharing me with my "school babies." Thank you also to the rest of my family (including those stalwart friends) who still encourage me to dream big, step outside of the box, and take chances in life and with my heart. Be good.

CONTENTS

List of Figures.. v

List of Reproducible Forms.. v

INTRODUCTION An Ode to 2020 and the Pandora's Box It Opened 1

Using This Book to Respond to Students in Crisis.................................... 3

    Four Sources of Student Trauma 4

    A Call to Action.. 6

CHAPTER 1 The Self/Home: Latent Trauma 7

Layers of Trauma in Students' Lives.. 7

Recognizing Student Trauma 9

Action Items for Updating Response Procedures for Self/Home-Based Trauma.... 10

    Building Strong Connections with Students and Families 12

    Communicating Trauma Procedures to Staff 16

    Collecting Data to Assess Student Needs 18

Chapter Summary 19

CHAPTER 2 The School: Incorporated Trauma 21

The Importance of an Effective Crisis Team 22

Action Items for Updating Response Procedures for School-Based Trauma 25

    Bolstering Your Crisis Team Members and Establishing a Calendar........... 27

    Is Your Trauma Kit Ready?.. 29

    Informed Practices 31

Chapter Summary 32

CHAPTER 3 The City: Sizeable Trauma 35

The Perpetual Fallout from Community Stress 36

Action Items for Updating Response Procedures for Citywide Trauma 37

    Mapping the Community 39

    Reaching Out to Your Community.. 40

    Sharing Resources with Students.. 42

Chapter Summary 44

CHAPTER 4 The State/Country/World: Mass-Scale Trauma 45

Tailoring Comprehensive Trauma Interventions for Individual Students 46

Action Items for Updating Response Procedures for Mass-Scale Trauma 48

    The Importance of Educators' Presence 49

    Preparedness for a Quick Move 50

    Intentional Practices: Teaching SEL and Mindfulness 53

Chapter Summary 54

Spotlight: Supporting Military-Connected Students 57

Recommended Resources 65

Index 69

About the Author 73

LIST OF FIGURES

Figure 1.0 The Sources of Student Trauma 5

Figure 1.1 Example of the Layers of Student Trauma 8

Figure 1.2 Signs of Trauma and Stress 9

Figure 1.3 Action Items for Self/Home-Based Trauma 11

Figure 1.4 Sample Script for a Family Conversation 14

Figure 1.5 Important Resources for a Trauma Response Guide 17

Figure 2.1 Action Items for School-Based Trauma 26

Figure 2.2 Sample Schedule for Crisis Team Meetings 28

Figure 2.3 Items to Include in a Trauma Kit 30

Figure 3.1 Action Items for Citywide Trauma 38

Figure 3.2 Create a Community Map 40

Figure 3.3 Identify Community Supports 41

Figure 4.1 Sample Individualized Intervention for Mass-Scale Trauma 47

Figure 4.2 Action Items for Mass-Scale Trauma 49

Figure 4.3 Sample Schoolwide Plans for Various Circumstances 51

Figure 4.4 Sample Contents of a Master Information Binder 52

LIST OF REPRODUCIBLE FORMS

See page 71 for instructions for downloading digital versions of these forms.

Teacher Quick Sheet for Trauma Response 58

Trauma Response Preparations Worksheet for School Planning 60

Action Items At-a-Glance 62

AN ODE TO 2020 AND THE PANDORA'S BOX IT OPENED

The COVID-19 pandemic hit the world hard. Sometimes it feels like it was the opening show to one of the most challenging years we have ever experienced. In the same way that I started looking around my house and noticing things that needed fixing, perhaps the quarantine-induced stillness revealed obstacles in our society that had always bubbled below the surface but remained covered by busy, moving schedules. Either way, recent months have been turbulent to say the least. We are still paddling our way out of deep waters, and the future remains very uncertain. If we have learned anything, however, it is that the connections we foster and the ways we support each other make all the difference, especially in the darkest of times.

In the days that followed the announcement of the school closures, many educators connected with colleagues, parked alone in front of our empty schools and cried, had comforting staff meetings on Zoom, and began to imagine our identities as teachers, counselors, administrators, coaches, and specialists outside of the school building. Then, we got down to business.

Like other industries during the pandemic wave, we had to figure out how to adapt to many new challenges, and fast. Along with healthcare, education stood out among the most resilient professions. Within days, many of us had schedules, online spaces, meetings, spreadsheets, and a plan. These early days and the weeks that followed were not without flaws, but not for lack of effort. I was in such awe with my own administrative team and the teachers I am so lucky to work with, it almost felt like an out-of-body experience. As if to not allow the adults to outdo them, many of our young students responded in spades as well. Some joined us digitally, some completed work on their own, some contacted their teachers through TikTok! Even for those students and school districts that faced additional obstacles to digital learning, the heart and intense dedication were there.

Behind the scenes of high-intensity situations like this, our brains work in overdrive to process our thoughts and emotions. Strength and grit will only take us so far as we try to develop understanding. In time, our students often sat silently in virtual lunch bunches begging us not to end the video calls because they just wanted to be together in some capacity. They started to message us about their sadness, and we began to get reports of children and families struggling to endure.

I've heard stories about people getting hit by cars and standing up immediately afterward, only to collapse when the body's adrenaline slows down—allowing their minds to register the pain from broken bones. Similarly, the excitement of adapting to the pandemic situation began to wear off and we started to feel the full effects of what was actually happening. Institutions our lives had always been based on simply stopped, social interactions that got us from one day to another were no more, and safety felt far out of reach. We were suffering and so were our students.

And then, as we were reeling from the pandemic, we took another huge fall. This time, the problem was not a virus, it was us. While we watched the police murder of George Floyd in horror, and witnessed and/or participated in mass protests, historic patterns of inequality and racism were laid bare. Our country as a whole began to fully register the reality that years of implicit, and often explicit, systemic racism has been allowed to control the masses and destroy the lives of our Black, Indigenous, and People of Color (BIPOC) citizens. It is tragic to think of the progress our society could have made over the decades by more strongly supporting BIPOC students—and future leaders—and guiding White students to understand racism and become anti-racist.

How are our students coping with such large-scale traumas that envelop them as they try to make sense of their world and discover their identities? These large-scale crises are eclipsing all of the usual crises young people already endure and must make approaching adulthood seem daunting, if not impossible.

How are our students coping with such large-scale traumas that envelop them as they try to make sense of their world and discover their identities?

I know I am not alone in believing that educators are here to help change the course of history. When we give our students a voice and a platform, they are able to grow into adults who will lead our country and world in meaningful and impassioned ways. With our guidance and belief, they will renew *our* hope in the ability of humans to create an equitable and just world. Our students deserve our care and understanding of what they have already been through and of the traumas they are currently experiencing. After all, one might say that we adults are the root of the problem for allowing such health threats and societal tensions to rise to this point in the first place.

What have I learned personally from the trauma I have experienced in recent months? Sometimes, big things happen—and not just one at a time. Sometimes, we can work really hard to plan and prepare, and things can still fall apart. When these crises arise, we cannot go back to the way things were before, and that can feel sad and scary. What we *can* do is adapt (even if slowly), and once we allow the fog to clear, we can find solace inside the spaces we have created in our own minds and hearts. And perhaps most importantly, *nobody* is in this alone.

> Everything can be taken from a [person] but one thing: the last of the human freedoms—to choose one's attitude in any given set of circumstances, to choose one's own way.
> —Viktor E. Frankl

Using This Book to Respond to Students in Crisis

As I write this, the upcoming 2020–2021 school year will present unique challenges in terms of traumatization for our students. They have been on a rough road together, experiencing a global pandemic, terrifying medical warnings, international community upheaval, and explicit messages confirming that racism is not only a powerful and destructive force in our society, but a real, physical threat for countless children and teens. Do we know of a time when the sneeze of a classmate could elicit anxious feelings? How will our Black students feel, in the wake of Floyd's murder and ongoing protests, walking into schools and classrooms surrounded by the authority of mostly White teachers and principals? What feelings or interactions will arise within conversations between students at a time when emotions and fears are so raw and exposed?

One of the major distinctions between school counselors and other counseling and educational professions is our understanding of mental health within the learning environment. This expertise allows us to aid students in the development of their emotional health, which is necessary for knowledge acquisition and overall growth. We believe that students achieve the greatest success when the whole person is strong and fit. The biggest obstacle to this work by far is student trauma.

I often tell people that I believe school counseling is more of an education philosophy than a profession. Though school counselors are trained specifically for their role in mental health, their aim is for students to be socially and emotionally healthy so they can be the best learners they can be. Unfortunately, not all schools have the funding for supportive roles such as school counselors and social workers. Although I believe we provide a clear and measurable value to the educational environment, many teachers and administrators bear the burden of both the academic instruction and the emotional development of the children they serve. Hence, this book is designed to be used by all educators, providing tools for planning trauma responses that can be used by a wide variety of staff members, whomever they may be.

I like to picture student development as a complex, living system. A growing child exercises various parts within this system, such as mental health, physical health, motivation, learning, and recall. The overall developmental goal is to attain alignment and balance for adult life through experiential learning and social and emotional support. When one of the system's parts is stressed because of traumatic experiences, it will pull energy from the other parts to fill the void. A student in crisis, for example, will likely feel helpless and confused. As their head works on their heart, a gap forms in their education because the trauma sucks energy away from the motivation and attention they need to learn. The purpose of using trauma responses with students is to help young people process their experiences, repair the damage to their mental health, and bring their system back into balance.

> **The purpose of using trauma responses with students is to help young people process their experiences, repair the damage to their mental health, and bring their system back into balance.**

Four Sources of Student Trauma

The four primary sources of student trauma discussed in this book are the child's *self/home*, *school*, *city*, and *state/country/world*. Events and struggles in each of these environments have the potential to harm a student's well-being and mental processes in different ways. This book explores each source of trauma and presents focused techniques that can be used specifically within that area. The techniques can also be used together to create more customized options.

The goal is to achieve fluidity in our trauma response practices so we can individualize strategies when responding to specific traumatic events and to students' specific needs. Each chapter has specified action items that you can implement immediately and use as a step-by-step guide to revamp your trauma response procedures across the four sources of trauma. The action items build on each other so that by the end of the book, you will have a comprehensive, collaborative, and updated trauma response program.

As you read, keep students' ages in mind when using the examples provided as models for training and practice. Though the basic actions suggested for revamping your trauma protocols would work for a range of elementary and secondary levels, it's crucial to consider age and population when making decisions about communication and lesson planning.

Figure 1.0 The Sources of Student Trauma

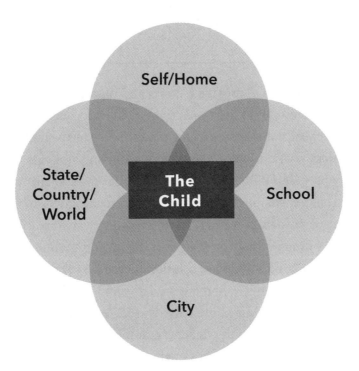

There is no quick fix when working with students who are experiencing the emotional domino effects of traumatic events, but there is the possibility of a well-orchestrated long game. Some key questions we need to ask to understand and respond to trauma include:

- What are the sources of trauma?

- What information is helpful for our mental health practitioners to have?

- What plans need to be in place to address traumatic events?

- What resources need to be provided in a crisis response kit?

- How can various staff members help address student trauma together?

- How do we plan for unknown crises that might arise in the future?

As you read, reflect on the students you work with so you can begin the conversation on how best to support them in your school (or even other workplaces).

By focusing on mental health in any environment, we can support everyone and live healthier lives. As you construct your response plan, provide training, and solidify schedules, think about ways that you can weave social and emotional learning and trauma-informed care into the framework of how you already operate. Be ready to respond to different types of trauma in different spheres, make concrete protocols to support your colleagues, and, ultimately, help provide harmony in your building even if the backyard is in chaos.

A Call to Action

The purpose of this book is to provide a linear and organized way to view trauma exposure in our schools and to help you create clear and concise protocols for responding to the needs of students during crisis. The heartbeat of each school is driven by countless relationships and interactions among students, staff, families, and community partners. With so many opportunities for student support within this complex structure, sometimes breaking our protocols down to the smallest parts reminds us of the details we may have forgotten over time.

The year 2020 brought the world some of the most tumultuous times we have ever seen. Luckily, educators are solution-focused. We know that the road ahead of us is going to be tough, and our students and families need us to help them heal from the traumas they have experienced. We also know that we will be ready to the very best of our ability. Teachers, administrators, specialists, school counselors, office associates, cafeteria servers, security teams, and custodial staff all devote their careers to children and will put in the hard work to make a plan that will allow us to support our students. We are not the only resource for our families, but we are an integral part of community-based services that can work collaboratively for children.

Just as we remain pillars for our students, a sturdy trauma protocol can support school staff in times of crisis. Adults are not safe from the harmful effects of witnessing and experiencing trauma. Hopefully, the framework provided in the following sections will also help school staff feel secure at work.

Together, we can work to bring light to dark situations, and be each other's inspiration for creating brighter times ahead.

The action items in this book can be accomplished by any school staff member who is knowledgeable about trauma response. This might include someone on the school leadership team, school counselors, or teachers. As with any effort, however, there is strength in numbers. Everyone can play a part and evaluate these procedures to offer each school the most comprehensive perspective on the trauma affecting its students and the task of identifying student needs. Together, we can work to bring light to dark situations, and be each other's inspiration for creating brighter times ahead.

CHAPTER 1

THE SELF/HOME: LATENT TRAUMA

Examples of trauma within the self/home: mental illness; crisis in the home; experiences with prejudice; violence or abuse in the family; loss of housing/resources; substance abuse; serious illness, injury, or death of a family member; struggles with identity; lack of medical attention.

When we think of trauma, we often point to external, exposed moments of crisis like a death in the family, abrupt divorce, or a singular violent event. We have a tangible idea of what emotions the student might be grappling with, such as loss or hurt, and we can make clear plans to help support the student. Sometimes, though, trauma is more latent and beneath the surface. We might not immediately recognize the emergence of a mental health disorder or experiences with racism. In these more systemic traumatic situations, trauma creeps quietly and is normalized over time, making the source less identifiable. Educators are tasked with keeping a keen eye on student behavior to be able to respond swiftly and ensure the safety of the student by finding them support.

Layers of Trauma in Students' Lives

Larger traumatic events trickle down through the spheres of a student's world to create layers of trauma. For example, during the COVID-19 pandemic, we know that students may be experiencing anxiety and dread over the distressing images they are seeing in the media as they watch overloaded hospitals and widespread illness. They know they are living in a world in peril. As the fallout reaches local communities, students may see more particular crises through medical care shortages and unavailability of community resources that they have come to depend on (like school, sports, social clubs, worship services, and food banks), creating feelings of fear for their family and their own safety and wellness.

With the unprecedented school closures, we have seen students lose hope and feel isolated and depressed when this community pillar is no longer accessible. For some students, being at home all the time may also mean increased exposure to violence and physical or mental abuse, the effects of strained economic resources, or physical or mental illness within their own home, causing extreme stress and hopelessness. This stress, in turn, magnifies the individual trauma a student may already be experiencing, such as anxiety, depression, special needs diagnoses, self-esteem issues, peer cruelty, or changes relating to puberty. These layers of trauma echo the four sources of trauma discussed earlier: the self/home, school, city, and state/country/world. It is important to note that during these times of global crisis, it's impossible to treat each layer separately; we must be responding to student trauma of all types from all sources, and our responses should build on one another. For example, if there is trauma in a school, we must address the group trauma as well as the trauma of individuals directly involved. In doing so, the student is enveloped in support by the layered efforts of trauma response occurring within the school.

Figure 1.1 Example of the Layers of Student Trauma

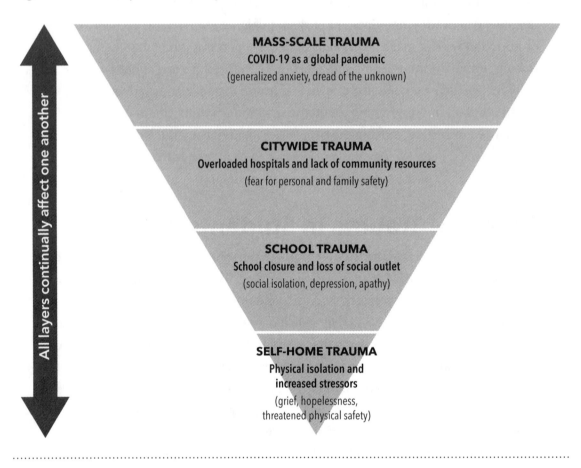

When a large group of people are struggling with trauma, you can feel the palpable weight of their struggle. With the disparities that our nation and world have experienced while enduring the COVID-19 pandemic, financial hardship, and widespread unrest in response to systemic racism, it is safe to say that the next several years will find students entering our hallways in a heavy fog of concern. They will have grown, they will have endured hardship, and they will likely still be struggling. The relative security that some felt before these impactful events will be forever altered. We will need to diligently observe student behavior and be careful not to minimize their actions or shut them down with comments alleging "attention-seeking drama" in order to help them before their emotions manifest into destructive outlets.

Recognizing Student Trauma

Oftentimes, when a student experiences trauma in their personal life, they show tell-tale signs of struggling. Abrupt changes in behavior and chronic fatigue are natural body responses that students often do not even realize are happening. Sometimes, however, student behavior changes are less noticeable (like obsessive questioning) or done with a smile (like overly playful behavior in the classroom). Whether students exhibit obvious or less obvious responses to trauma, it is important to address these changes.

Figure 1.2 Signs of Trauma and Stress

Obvious Signs of Trauma and Stress	Less Obvious Signs of Trauma and Stress
• Swift drop in grades • Despondency • Detachment from peers • Sleepiness or lethargy • Abrupt attendance change • Skipping meals and loss of appetite • Mood changes/emotional outbursts	• Lingering around the counselor's office • Less interest in hobbies • Bouts of daydreaming • Increased requests to call home • Loitering in the bathrooms • Increased obsession with order • Constant questioning/double-checking

Sometimes, a school is unaware of a student's traumatic experience. In these cases, student behavior often feels like it comes out of nowhere. For example, the quiet student who has always been able to avoid the spotlight by sitting politely in the back of the room gets into a fight in the locker room, or the boisterous student who disrupts their way through class comes to school one day with scabbed lines on their arms. These students may not have strong connections with adults in their school—some children avoid relationships with staff as learned self-defense or as a safeguard of family secrets. Though no one may have seen their behavior as it changed, swift trauma protocol can be used to establish trusting connection and find interventions to help these students.

I always appreciate when a teacher sends me a message to check on a student who "seems off." Many times, I find that there is indeed something below the surface that I would not otherwise have seen. A student who has stopped socializing and appears lethargic during class, for example, might come to my office and disclose that their grandparent who has always lived in the home is now in hospice. With a busy caretaking parent and a student unable to verbalize their sadness, the school would likely have had no idea that anything was going on at home. Without that "heads up" from the observant teacher, I would not have had the opportunity to create support through something so heavy and life-changing.

The very reason social and emotional learning (SEL) is essential in the educational environment is that it is often in school that emotions are unearthed. It is difficult to process traumatic events in the introspective and orderly school environment as students try to move through the day struggling with focus, feeling isolated from their peers, and carrying the weight of their secrets.

The collective positive rapport and established trust with students becomes our window to assisting a student in crisis.

When a student starts to process the magnitude of whatever anguish they are experiencing, the school community reaches a pivotal moment together. All of the hard work that the teachers, school counselors, administrators, specialists, teacher assistants, and office workers have put into making connections comes together. The collective positive rapport and established trust with students becomes our window to assisting a student in crisis. This is a critical first step in responding to any student experiencing trauma, making it easier to assess the situation and begin to gather data for responding.

Action Items for Updating Response Procedures for Self/Home-Based Trauma

The action items below can assist any school in developing or updating a fundamental trauma response protocol. These are largely tasks that the school as a whole can utilize and benefit from while navigating times of crises with students. It is best if a central group of staff (usually administration, school counselors, and/or teacher leaders) establishes norms and practices for the school, and then creates dynamic training opportunities for the collective staff. However, you can identify your "power players" based on what resources are available to you within your district or school. If necessary, an individual teacher can create their own trauma response protocol for their classroom and teaching practice.

Figure 1.3 Action Items for Self/Home-Based Trauma

Protocol	Goal	Trauma Response Update Ideas
Calling Home	*Ensure there is a protocol for calling home for trauma inquiries.*	• Provide professional development (PD) on family communication. • Use specific activities to teach the protocol in PD groups.
Relationship Building	*Allow time for building relationships with students throughout the day.*	• Evaluate staff schedules to allow time for relationship building. • Create mentorships, check-ins/outs, and/or advisory programs.
Emergency Numbers	*Emphasize mandated reporting requirements and ensure all staff have community emergency numbers.*	• Provide handouts to post in each classroom. • Include the information in PD.
School Trauma Response	*Establish a schoolwide trauma response protocol and make sure staff are up-to-date.*	• Provide a copy to each teacher for the classroom and include it in all substitute teacher folders. • Construct PD workshops using sample scenarios.
Needs Assessments	*Create assessments and collect data to find out what your students need.*	• Determine the assessment's purpose and create assessments within PD groups. • Use assessment data in PD workshops to address student needs.

The very least of trauma response in schools is a thoughtful protocol for responding to students in crisis. Rules and actions should be clearly stated and transparent for staff. Most schools already have this protocol on some level, but due to the rapid changes our students have experienced in recent months, revamping these policies and procedures may be in order. Some of it will remain the same, and some of our protocols will look much different. For example, with the absence of hugs and whispered confidentiality—and even smiles while staff and students wear masks—we will need to rethink expressions of care.

Building Strong Connections with Students and Families

Rapport building is much like saving money. Each tiny interaction we have with a student provides an opportunity for them to feel heard and cared for.

> **Each tiny interaction we have with a student provides an opportunity for them to feel heard and cared for.**

Remembering something personal about them, offering a snack, sharing an inside joke, and smiling or waving are all tiny deposits that go into that individual account. Alone, these simple actions might seem trivial, but together they are an investment that you make in the work you and the student do together over time or in a time of crisis. The key to building relationships is staying the course. This means continuing to put in this effort even when students do not respond warmly, or when you cannot see the investment growing.

Calling home is one of the easiest actions an educator can take to build stronger relationships with students. In my own practice, I love calling home because I get to learn more about family dynamics, and if the parent is willing to work with me on school-based initiatives for their child, I also get to show the student that we are a united front. In most cases, the more a family approves of me, the more a student sees me as an integrated part of their life. Sometimes, this requires delicate individual conversations with students, parents, and other staff members to try to bring everyone to a better understanding of each other. For example, if a student is struggling after revealing a sexual orientation that their parents do not accept, I can work on identity development and self-advocacy with the student, while providing resources and perspective to the parent. The relationships we make with parents and students are not independent, but rather tethered to each other in an attempt to bring them both to a healthy meeting place.

Stakeholders coming together in support is important for all students, and especially important for students in homes that are struggling with unstable housing, food insecurity, contentious divorce, or domestic violence. In the aftermath of the many recent events in the United States and abroad, hardships such as these have multiplied. Creating a collaborative environment that the student might be craving can be done by reaching out. When calling home to explore possible sources of trauma, try to do the following:

1. **Begin with a general check-in.** Ask the parent or guardian how everything is going and open up a lighter dynamic in the conversation so the parent doesn't build quick defense mechanisms. Most parents are trying their best, and constantly receiving negative phones calls can be defeating. We want to earn their trust.

2. **Discuss something you love about their child.** Leading with positive qualities and showing how well you know their child will mean a lot to a parent who feels exhausted from having to constantly advocate for their child's needs. We have to distinguish ourselves from other hardships or prejudices parents have experienced and dealt with in their lives.

3. **Consistently check in with your own feelings, even as you discuss the behavior in question.** Are you reporting the behavior because it is attention-seeking and you hope there are consequences at home, or are you reporting the behavior because you know there is something deeper going on? If you feel that you are calling in anger, you are not alone! However, though we are in one of the most taxing professions, we are responsible for processing our personal frustrations and returning to a place of concern before addressing an issue with a parent.

4. **Let the parents know you are concerned and why.** Align your intentions to be centered on healing. Make it clear that you are seeking advice to create a solution.

5. **Listen.** The source of trauma might be expressed, or you may need to read between the lines of what a struggling parent is saying. Just, *really* listen. If they react with anger, listen. If they cry, listen. If they are exasperated, listen. The seed of injury is in there somewhere, and the goal is to identify it and assist before it takes over.

6. **Ask the parent how they feel.** When a student experiences trauma, so too does their family. When we are holistically student-centered, we know part of that is a stable home life. This is not to say that a teacher or counselor can take on the weight of qualified social service agents or mental health counselors. But sometimes, just asking someone if they are okay can offer a friendly ray of hope during a difficult time.

> The relationships we make with parents and students are not independent, but rather tethered to each other in an attempt to bring them both to a healthy meeting place.

7. **Make a plan that includes solicited advice from the parent.** Tell the parent you have some ideas for how you can support the student at school but be explicit in pointing out that as the parent, they know their child better than anyone else. Strategies like check-ins, teacher team meetings, journal time, and quiet lunches with the counselor might help a parent feel reassured and help the student feel like the school environment is more manageable while they are in distress.

Always remember that people are *doing the best they can with the tools that they have*. This has long been my guiding light in education (and in everyday life). Remembering this tenet of counseling helps shed bias and judgment that might get in the way of a family or student getting assistance. It is not about putting yourself in the parent's shoes as much as it is about accepting who they are and the path that has brought them to your office or classroom. They want what is best for their child, they just may need extra tools in their toolbox.

We might know how best to teach a child, but that is because we went to school and were trained in this area. Someone who has not been taught these strategies and theories of learning can't be expected to know this content. They are, however, the expert on their child, and it is important to let them know that this makes them our greatest resource in the work that we can do with their student. Building trusting relationships with their parents strengthens the relationships we can make with our students because it helps us get know them and is an efficient way to establish their needs.

School counselors have a bit of a secret toolbox that we use when we talk to parents. Our counseling classes are all about ensuring that the client feels safe enough to be open and honest. This is incredibly helpful when calling home to parents, especially when sensitive topics need to be discussed. By inviting your counseling team to share these tools with the larger staff, teachers can feel more comfortable and have more productive conversations when they call home. For schools that do not have school counselors, the crisis team and/or administration can provide staff with basic information on "interviewing skills" fundamentals.

Let's look at a sample conversation with an exasperated parent who gets a phone call regarding their child's grades, and break down some secret tools for a productive outcome:

Figure 1.4 Sample Script for a Family Conversation

Speaker	Dialogue	Tools and Tips
Teacher	Hello, Mrs. Blain, I hope you are doing well. I know there is so much going on lately–it has been quite hectic!	*Frontload from a place of concern.*
Parent	I'm okay. I've tried to call the school several times and no one has answered.	

Teacher	I'm sorry, it has been so busy since returning to school. This morning I was actually looking through my list of students who have dropped their grades and I did notice Brian's name in there. I know how well he was doing, so I'm thinking this is new. I'm wondering if you could think of anything that might be bugging him, or any way I can help?	*State your overall goal so they know you're not singling out their child.* *Avoid "why" questions that appear accusatory.*
Parent	Are you kidding me?! Why is this the first I have heard about this?	
Teacher	I know, sometimes it does creep up quickly. When I left a message a bit ago, I knew I should have followed up with an email because it has been such a chaotic time.	*Do not interpret their frustration as criticism.*
Parent	Well, we were getting a million calls and emails from the school. I can't keep up with everything. These schedules keep changing. Do you really expect me to hold him accountable for his schoolwork when he's only there part of the time? If the school is not going to listen when I say these new schedules are not going to work, I'm not going to make him do anything. I told him no one is going to hold this against him.	
Teacher	Oh my goodness, I completely understand your frustration. I can hardly tell which way is up these last few weeks. He seemed to be keeping up with everything very well for a while. Then all of a sudden he stopped doing the digital component work at home. He hasn't really talked to me about anything going on, have you noticed changes at home as well?	*Show understanding.* *Make it clear you respect that they are expert on their child.*
Parent	Obviously, his grades have gone down! He missed all that time last year when the schools shut down! I'm not a teacher, I can only do so much, and all of the assignments were way too confusing, it was ridiculous! Isn't that your job? I told you I'm not making him do anything. I was yelling at him because I was so frustrated but then he would get upset and I finally told him to just forget about it!	*Try to sense when the parent is feeling overwhelmed or inadequate and validate their emotions.*
Teacher	I completely understand, you parents have had so much on your plates. I can tell you have been working hard to support him at home. I cannot change the schedules or the circumstances, but maybe there is something I can do to help? What are your thoughts on him staying after school so I can go over some of the assignments with him? Or I can set up digital meetings whenever it is convenient for you two? Do you think it would be helpful?	*Avoid saying, "Do you want me to . . ." because it insinuates that they don't want what is best for their student.* *Emphasize the strong team the parent(s) and students make.*

Parent	I don't even get home until after 6:00! Fine, he can stay after, but I don't have room to remember one more thing! You'll have to remind him. I hardly see him at all since I was furloughed and had to take a second job and work three mornings a week. If it is Wednesdays, you'll have to call his dad. We separated last year and that is his day for visitation.	*Take note when the parent gives you the "aha moment" and lets you in on the sources of the problem.*
Teacher	I am so sorry to hear that. Wow, you have so much going on! It's no problem. I will talk to him today, if it's okay with you, and we will pick a day. I'll be sure to email you so we all know the plan. I will provide you with the digital meeting details if he prefers to do it online, or he can ride the activity bus home, so you won't even have to pick him up!	*Use "we" instead of "you" to show partnership.* *Take the weight off of their shoulders to show you are simply looking to help.*
Parent	Yes. Yes, actually that would be great. I'm just frustrated, I know it's not your fault. I just don't know what else to do and I don't feel like I'm good at teaching him this stuff. The divorce and furlough have been hard.	
Teacher	Please don't apologize, you're doing a great job. If it's okay with you I'd love to let the school counselor know. She's great, and I think she would speak with Brian and see if he'd like to talk or just have a place to go.	*After earning trust, refer to trauma specialists.*
Parent	Yes please. I've been meaning to call but I haven't had the time.	

Communicating Trauma Procedures to Staff

Though home-based trauma varies greatly, procedures for responding to an underlying or concealed crisis can still be established and easily provided through rapport that has been built with parents, guardians, and students. With our industry's extensive history of compassion to lean on, schools can help by providing busy teachers with easy-to-follow procedures.

When a student experiences trauma or is in a crisis situation, it is an emergency. Each school should have an easy-access guidebook with protocols for responding to students experiencing trauma in their lives. The table on page 17 lists important resources a trauma response guide should include, along with questions your team should be addressing about these resources.

When a student experiences trauma or is in a crisis situation, it is an emergency.

Figure 1.5 Important Resources for a Trauma Response Guide

Resource	Questions to Ask
Local emergency contacts and phone numbers	Have your staff been told explicitly that all staff in contact with students should call Child Protective Services to report suspected child abuse? Staff should: <ul><li>have access to non-emergency and emergency phone numbers or hotlines to report abuse</li><li>feel comfortable calling abuse or suicide hotlines if it is suspected that a child is in danger</li><li>know who to contact if they have concerns about the well-being of a student</li></ul>
Professionals in the school who are trained to respond to crisis situations	Do you have access to school counselors and/or school social workers, and do staff know what those colleagues are trained for? Staff should: <ul><li>be aware of resources within the school who are experts in child trauma and crisis welfare</li><li>know about resources and trainings offered within the district in the event that they have a question or concern</li><li>be provided basic information on trauma and the way the brain works when a child is in distress</li></ul>
Established timeline of contact with administrators, counselors, and families	How quickly should a school counselor or administrator be contacted when there is a suspicion of a student in crisis? How quickly should a call home be made? Staff should: <ul><li>know who they need to call in the event that they sense a student may be experiencing a crisis</li><li>know who can assist them with calling home</li><li>be provided ample training on guidelines for calling home</li></ul>
Explicit directions for documenting contact and intervention plans	Where should all contacts for the student be reported so that all staff members in contact with the student can see what kind of support the family needs while still respecting their confidentiality? Staff should: <ul><li>be provided a confidential place to document all contact made to the student, family, and school leadership</li><li>have training in confidentiality protocols</li><li>be notified when school leadership meets on interventions so they can know how to proceed with their own plans with the student</li></ul>

NOTE: It cannot be stressed enough that if any adult feels that a student is in danger of harming themselves or others, local emergency services should be called before anything else. Immediate danger is a game changer. All educators are mandated reporters and should ensure they know how to contact Child Protective Services, emergency hotlines, and/or non-emergency 911.

If you are a teacher using this book as a framework to create your own protocols for responding to trauma within your classroom and find that you have not been given answers to these questions from your school leadership, now is a great time to advocate within your school! Asking your administration for answers to emergency planning may also signify to them that it is time to update the professional development practices in your school.

Collecting Data to Assess Student Needs

Needs assessments have long been an important part of education. They help us gain a window into our population so that we know what resources are needed most. There are many types of needs assessments, and they can be layered over time to give a systemic picture of what students are lacking. You can collect data with questionnaires (such as Google Forms), meeting notes, check-in/out documentation, entrance/exit slips, or even raising of hands surveying in the classroom. The goal is to be able to see where everyone is and what needs exist, but also to have a way to monitor any changes or patterns.

The goal is to be able to see where everyone is and what needs exist, but also to have a way to monitor any changes or patterns.

Sometimes, like recently with the mass-scale collective traumas, we already have a baseline of possible concerns that might be affecting our students. The next step then is to see how these issues boil down to the individual home. Though all our students may have had a fear for their health or their family's health, for example, how has the COVID-19 pandemic affected their family life privately? Appraisals of student needs might include the following goals:

- **Assess collected data with "at risk" caseload lists.** Before students are in the building, take a deep dive into their data to create tiers of response. Students who struggle with grades, have poor attendance, or have extensive behavioral records might be experiencing trauma; these are well-established signifiers. You can begin to determine who might be high-need and get to know them through their data before getting the chance to establish rapport. This is a great place to also mark other known risk factors such as high mobility, difficulties with learning, military connectedness, or history of grade retention.

- **Assess fluid data as you work with student focus groups.** Focus groups are subgroups of our caseloads or student bodies that are composed of students with a specified risk factor. These groups are perfect for data collection through the tracking of interventions that are individualized for each student. Interventions might include check-ins, collaboration between counselors and teachers for all-encompassing support, and watching data points for grades, attendance, and behavior for quick intervention. Sometimes I like to keep a focus group of students whose parents reach out to me asking for extra support for their children because of a known crisis; other times I might have a focus group of students who have failed a class, for which one of my goals is to discover a root of their issue. I was lucky to receive mentorship with my focus group this year after my school administration asked that counselors in my school include focus groups as an annual professional goal. We worked together on evaluating and adjusting student interventions throughout the year. In doing so, I was able to tailor my work with my focus group students as their lives and experiences changed. You might consider such mentorship or partnership for your school.

- **Assess provided data with questionnaires.** Technology has made needs assessments easier than ever before. With various survey tools, we can now poll our families for needs and collect quick data that can be used to shape specified trauma training and protocols for each school. Asking families to provide information on their homes allows schools to better provide resources and parent outreach opportunities.

Chapter Summary

Young people may experience many different layers of trauma at once. They are observing their overwhelming surroundings while also trying to make sense of who they are and what role they play in the larger society. Their world begins in the personal realm of the self and home before radiating to the school, their local community, and larger geographic areas. By parsing out each sphere of impact, we are able to create an all-inclusive system of support for students who have experienced traumatic events. When there are needs in the self/home sphere, the student will come to school with a deficit. We can reach out and stay connected to our students and families to help establish our place as a safe space. We can also share emergency information and specific trauma response guidelines with staff and collect data to inform us of the unique needs of students in our schools.

LOOKING AHEAD . . .

Next up, we will build on our knowledge of responding to trauma in a student's self/home sphere with rapport building and data collection by taking a look at the student's second home: the school. Here, students may experience trauma together, adding both benefits and drawbacks to how crises are processed. A well-organized crisis team can quickly support the students and their families, provide community resources, offer resources within the school, and create a plan of action to ensure that students have persistent advocates as they begin to heal.

CHAPTER 2

THE SCHOOL: INCORPORATED TRAUMA

Examples of trauma within the school: serious illness, injury, or death of a student or staff member; peer violence; interpersonal issues with peers; relationship violence; school shooting; discrimination; abrupt school closures; severe and unplanned changes to the school environment or schedule.

When students enter their schools, they bring with them their traumatic experiences from home. Many of my students report feeling like the school is a place where they feel safe enough to be their true selves. We want our students to feel like their school is both an escape and a haven where they can express their emotions freely. When trauma is carried into a school or occurs onsite, the difficult emotions it produces can be directed or misdirected at any number of people the student interacts with at school (including themselves). When trauma is connected to the learning environment, a student may resist education for their whole life out of self-protection.

When trauma is connected to the learning environment, a student may resist education for their whole life out of self-protection.

To understand how far trauma can travel and how easily students can be exposed to trauma from peers, consider all the people the student comes into contact with at school. Detecting trauma exposure is much like the contact tracing we have come to be familiar with during the COVID-19 pandemic. Once you have a positive diagnosis of the disease, you work backwards to observe and test each person the patient has been in contact with. Similarly, a traumatic experience affects everyone the suffering child encounters. Students are social, and when they share their impactful experiences and feelings with friends, their peers become affected with worry as well. We are aiming to get as close as possible to the person experiencing the trauma firsthand so we can minimize widespread impact.

The Importance of an Effective Crisis Team

Working in a school and responding to student emotions can often feel like directing traffic at a busy intersection. There are feelings coming from many different directions, and the sources vary from child to child. We stand in the middle of them all, heads turning as we attempt to figure out who needs what and how fast. As a system, the staff within a school can include designated members that are prepared to respond to more intense traumatic situations and attempt to avoid as many collisions as possible.

A crisis event that occurs or comes into the school often alters the entire environment. When a teacher passes away, for example, individual students are affected, the teacher's class is affected, the staff are distressed, and the entire school's perspective and culture are disturbed. As students and staff attempt to process their feelings in the face of a traumatic event, a core team of staff members—a "crisis team"—can quickly fortify supportive structures so that the school can heal.

Ideally, a crisis team is made up of the school's administrative team, school counselors, and other student support staff such as school social workers and school psychologists. However, we know that not all districts have access to these in-school supports. A school may also have teachers and teacher's assistants who are knowledgeable about student trauma, or office staff who build relationships with students and families as they come in and out of the school. (*Note:* Those teachers who are using this book to create an individual classroom trauma response protocol can look to teachers in neighboring classrooms and accessible community members to create a crisis team that may be reached in a pinch.)

The key to a good crisis team is to identify staff members that have been trained in trauma response and are able to leave their role in the event of a crisis situation.

The key to a good crisis team is to identify staff members that have been trained in trauma response and are able to leave their role in the event of a crisis situation. This team is not solely operating in a counseling office setting. The crisis team should be an essential part of a school's ability to respond to students and staff experiencing trauma that also encourages the continued operation of the educational institution by allowing teachers to continue their work in the classroom.

Though every traumatic event will have different needs, clear and direct plans for responding to crisis events are essential. We cannot anticipate every crisis that may lie ahead, but we do know that our students have been exposed to significant trauma recently, and at some point we will experience additional trauma in our schools. This will be the case for every school-age child alive today, and for several years to come. Building a well-defined and trained crisis team will help ensure that before students walk into the building, they are supported.

Prior to beginning the year, it is important to make sure that the crisis team is familiar with needs assessment data, sources of trauma, and methods to avoid retraumatization when speaking with students who are in crisis. Let's look at two examples of crisis situations that a crisis team would be equipped to respond to.

Dennis is a third grader who comes to school on Monday and is sullen and unfocused in class. When the teacher asks him what is wrong, he says, "nothing," and she notices he will not make eye contact and avoids conversation. When he gets worked up while working in a group and loudly tells his classmate to shut up, the teacher tells him he needs to calm down and tries to speak with him privately to get a better idea of what is going on. When Dennis says he does not feel comfortable telling her, she tells him to go speak with the assistant principal.

The assistant principal senses something is bothering Dennis, so she sends him to the school counselor. Here, he is asked how his weekend went and he begins to cry. He says that on the bus on the way to school, some students used racist slurs towards him during a debate about the weekend baseball game. He said it was the first time he had faced "angry racism like that." He was scared and confused and is now struggling because he wonders how many other White people in his life feel the same way about him because of the color of his skin.

Sarah is a seventh grader who is sent to a counselor for mediation. A hall monitor overheard her saying what sounded like mean things to a friend about one of their other friends. The monitor noticed they also hadn't been sitting together at lunch and thinks there could be a fight brewing. Sarah is adamant that she does not want to talk to the other girl for mediation, and says that she has tried to fix things, but her friend will not listen. She says that she is worried she will get in trouble because she heard an adult say she and her friends were "just being mean girls," so she didn't know who to talk to.

After some coaxing, Sarah explains that the student she is estranged from is in a relationship that makes her uncomfortable. She says her friend's boyfriend gets really mad and yells at her when she talks to other boys, and he has been pressuring her to send him pictures of herself in a bathing suit or topless. When Sarah tried to get her friend to break up with him, her friend stopped talking to her. Sarah didn't understand why someone would think that they should be treated that way by anyone else. She thinks her friend might be in danger, but she felt if she told someone they would assume it was "girl drama."

Adults do not always assume that children are struggling with such heavy trauma as racial slurs and relationship violence. Sarah and Dennis are not only grappling with one traumatic event, they are also learning lessons about the ways that people can hurt one another. They have lost their innocence, and their whole worldview has been altered. As each individual student leans on their peers, so too will their peers be changed. You now have two singular, daunting incidents that will bleed down the hallway and transform a school.

Both Dennis and Sarah were reluctant to express their emotions due to racial and gender stereotypes they heard in the school, causing them instead to isolate themselves. Stereotypes can be reinforced in school by students and by staff. If we have learned anything in recent years, it is that dissolving implicit bias takes a great amount of work and honesty with each other and with ourselves, and it's a crucial component of anti-racism and progress toward a more equitable society. We have the power to unveil these discriminations within our schools. Shuffling Dennis off to the principal's office and using the term "mean girls" with Sarah caused these students to feel as though they could not reach out for help, reinforcing feelings of hopelessness due to racism and sexism.

One of the trickiest parts about being a school counselor is the way we ride the line between informing school staff about student personal lives and upholding the confidentiality codes that we are trained to adhere to. In a community counseling office, it is easier to maintain the confidentiality of clients. In school counseling, however, we need to find ways to support students from many facets of their lives to help them achieve social emotional and educational growth, while still respecting the essential privacy of the client. The goal is to find a balance that lets us inform others of a student's needs without exploiting their situation, breaking their trust, or risking retraumatization while they are in school.

Sometimes, a teacher might benefit from having personal information about a student or a student's homelife, especially when the student is struggling with a traumatic situation. Consider a student whose housing is unstable due to abrupt economic hardship. The student will absolutely benefit from a caring and dedicated teacher, but the teacher can only be privy to so much information. This may likely be the case for many of our families following the sudden and unexpected closures due to COVID-19, which caused many parents and guardians to be laid off, furloughed, or placed on reduced work hours.

The balance between informing staff of student hardships and keeping student information confidential is important in ensuring that the school does not become a source of retraumatization for students. It is often difficult for students to talk about their emotions and the hardships they are experiencing. Sometimes this is because they have a difficult time putting their feelings into words and sometimes it is because they fear retribution for telling someone. If they are in the process of working through a traumatic situation and find out that an adult they confided in has discussed their private life with others, the school can then become another place that does not feel safe or secure.

> **The balance between informing staff of student hardships and keeping student information confidential is important in ensuring that the school does not become a source of retraumatization for students.**

Action Items for Updating Response Procedures for School-Based Trauma

Establishing a crisis team within a school not only helps support students as they continue learning in the educational environment, it also provides a smaller inner circle of people who can be aware of student needs and honor the confidentiality of their circumstances. Furthermore, ensuring crisis kits and crisis communication protocol are prepared offers a blueprint to school staff for quick and efficient response to traumatic situations. When all staff are aware of these processes, they are able to assist students effectively and with guidance from the crisis team.

Your crisis team needs to be knowledgeable about the signs of trauma response, types of trauma, and how to intervene in a crisis. They then become a rich resource to help staff members know the signs of trauma and retraumatization for quick intervention when necessary. Retraumatization is when someone's past traumatic experience is triggered, causing them to feel intense emotions associated with the initial impact of trauma. For example, a student who has lost a parent might be triggered by a simple assignment, reading passage, video, or friendly interaction. The trigger may come from out of nowhere and will typically take the student by surprise as much as anyone else. When this happens in middle school, the student typically leaves the classroom and reports later that they hadn't fallen apart like that in a long time, but just couldn't stop crying and didn't know why or what to do. In elementary school, you might likely find a student shutting down or reacting hyper-emotionally to small sensitivities.

Figure 2.1 Action Items for School-Based Trauma

Protocol	Goal	Trauma Response Update Ideas
Crisis Team	*Establish or bolster a crisis team and create a team meeting schedule.*	• Distribute to staff a list of crisis team members. • Schedule crisis team meetings and send invitations.
Trauma Kit	*Create a trauma kit to use in crisis situations that will aid in supporting students and families (see figure 2.3 on page 30 for items to include).*	• Research and add specific information about safety and wellness. • Research and add honest information about systemic racism and advocacy.
Statement Blueprints	*Prepare statements/scripts for emails, letters, and phone calls home to use in possible crisis situations.*	• Ensure the crisis team has input in and access to statements. • Provide teachers with statements for reference.
Scripts for Teachers	*Help teachers practice talking with parents about trauma.*	• Provide hard copy quick sheets to teachers. • Hold PD workshops with sample scenarios.

When an emotional wound from trauma is created or reopened in a student, it is essential that we properly attempt to heal the sore and reduce reoccurring exposure to the source of trauma. Children spend the better part of their young lives in their schools. Ideally, these are places of solace, comfort, and inclusive understanding. However, we cannot ignore the historic role schools have played in institutional racism and bigotry. Some schools are still based on the same divisive worldviews that others have worked so hard to break down. It is our responsibility to ensure that schools are enacting the civil rights reforms that all community institutions are being called on to accomplish. Our students need us to remind them that they are important and worthy. They need us to teach them that when you advocate for yourself and for others, you can make positive changes in policy and in people's lives.

> **Our students need us to remind them that they are important and worthy. They need us to teach them that when you advocate for yourself and for others, you can make positive changes in policy and in people's lives.**

Our students are hurting. We often have no idea what trauma they have witnessed in their personal lives. If we want students to engage and learn in the classroom, it has to feel like *their* classroom.

If BIPOC, gender-nonbinary, LGBTQ, special needs, and financially struggling students feel like outsiders in someone else's classroom, their learning will likely occur with struggle. These intense feelings of isolation and rejection in the school will become a new source of trauma, layering over the difficulties they are already experiencing at home. By creating and utilizing a crisis team and trauma response protocol, you can begin the process of integrating inclusive school policy and holding each other accountable. The year 2020 brought trials to masses of people like no other year in our memory, but with a little reinforcement and creativity, efforts of change and trauma response components will be an essential part of our practices in the years ahead.

Bolstering Your Crisis Team and Establishing a Calendar

The 2020 pandemic has shown schools just how important a crisis team and trauma response protocol can be. Some of us learned how to utilize our established programs, and some of us wished we had emergency plans in place to support students more quickly, or at all. Reinforcements to every school's current crisis team and protocols may be necessary with such changing times as we are seeing. How long will it take for students to process the anxiety caused by schools closing abruptly? What will happen in the future when students sit in class with a peer who has a cold? Likely, it will take a long time to edge worried minds back into calm minds focused on learning.

Some schools will need to reach out to their staff to construct a crisis team, and others can reinforce crisis teams that are already in place by assessing how equipped members are to respond to trauma and how knowledgeable they are about the school's climate and outside current events. Schools should also note whether the team has diverse representation and take steps to change that if it does not. Schedule regular meetings to share and update confidential information about struggling students. Ideally, changes to the crisis team and its roles should be made before the school year even starts, but as with any practice, efficiency should be evaluated throughout the year.

When a crisis team meets, they can share assessments of the school environment, developments related to trauma sources within the school, and information about specific family and student needs (confidentially). The team can then consult and brainstorm on how to best intervene and ease the repercussions of each crisis. This also provides school administration with a team of people that can offer professional development to the rest of the staff to help them better understand trauma and trauma response. Transparency around trauma protocols helps the entire staff feel supported and prepared in the event that they need to respond to an emergency situation.

Transparency around trauma protocols helps the entire staff feel supported and prepared in the event that they need to respond to an emergency situation.

Schools can work ahead by creating their crisis team calendar instead of waiting until signs of student need appear. We know that our students *are* in crisis and are *currently* experiencing trauma. The crisis team calendar and meeting notices ensure that everyone is able to attend each meeting, and they also send a message of priority to the team members. A long-term plan for crisis team meetings can be made so the team keeps its goals and focus. Special topics can be discussed at different meetings, and community experts can attend for continued learning when time allows. Following is a sample schedule.

Figure 2.2 Sample Schedule for Crisis Team Meetings

	September	October	November	December	January
1st week	Review trauma guide and protocols	Review student data	Speaker: local medical association	Review student data	Intervention brainstorming
3rd week	Staff PD prep	Assess bias in policy workshop	Staff PD prep	Discuss identified students	Speaker: local cultural association
	February	**March**	**April**	**May**	**June**
1st week	Review student data	Discuss teacher trauma survey	Review student data	Drop-out prevention alignment	Annual review of practices
3rd week	Staff PD prep	Review student mid-year questionnaire	Assess intervention success	Staff PD prep	Summer tasks and planning

An easy checklist for the crisis team might include:

- Schedule bi-weekly meetings to discuss students and cases.

- Ensure all school counselors and other student support staff members (if available) are part of the team and notified of the meetings.

- Ensure all administrators are on board.

- Include teachers who are interested in social and emotional learning or trauma recovery (especially if there are no school support staff members at the school).

- Consult with district leadership on any established protocols.

- Invite any specialists such as school social workers, mediation specialists, behavior specialists, special educators, etc.

- Build training into in-service professional development days for full transparency of the function of the team.

It is beneficial to have your crisis team review current policy to see what may need changing to better support students experiencing trauma due to exposed racism. For example, a teacher friend of mine raised the issue of the Confederate flag not being explicitly banned in district dress codes. Another has fought hard in her school to ease restrictions on headwear, such as hair wraps. Racism and discrimination are traumatizing. Racist protocols may not only trigger retraumatization for students and staff, but also hinder the hard work educators put into earning student trust. Students see rules as a representation of what the school and staff stand for, and if those rules are not in line with the equity your students deserve, they need a second look.

Is Your Trauma Kit Ready?

Trauma kits are used to respond to students experiencing crisis, as well as to readily offer tools and manipulatives to help students relax so they can talk about what they are feeling and experiencing. Your crisis team will need tools to be able to work with kids who are experiencing the byproducts of exposure to trauma. Items in the toolkit may include trauma procedures, intervention techniques, and scripts that might be helpful to staff members. These items are necessary when trauma hits a school, and you can get them ready now.

Due to the nature of various traumas that students are experiencing, we may also need to add another tool: information. Students are inundated with news on the internet containing intense imagery, shifting sources, and forceful opinions. They will have questions about questions on top of questions. It is essential for crisis teams interacting with struggling students to allow them space to speak and to be able to engage in conversations about current events. Crisis teams must be informed, and trauma kits should be equipped with informative and unbiased anti-racism materials.

A student who recognizes or calls out institutional racism will need reassurance that their school is working hard to combat racism and discrimination. But to simply state this is not enough. We can let students know that the school's crisis team is evaluating norms for bias, administrators are working on policy that is unbiased, and teachers are selecting inclusive material for lessons. In fact, students can be invited to play a role in these assessments so that we are not only hearing them but allowing them to show us as well.

It is essential that students feel ownership and authority over their feelings, and that their voices are heard. It's equally essential that crisis teams be equipped to offer information about history, progress, and ways to be an agent of change. Most importantly, the team must be prepared to have conversations without leading the student to a conclusion; a student's experience of trauma (whether it be domestic abuse, neighborhood crime, riots, spread of serious illness at school, death of a teacher, or bigotry) is their truth.

Figure 2.3 Items to Include in a Trauma Kit

Double-check that the following items are ready to go:	
Trauma Procedures	Make sure your trauma procedures are up-to-date and accessible in hard copy.
Crisis Team	Provide a list of all crisis team members, in case backup is needed or coordinated support for a student or staff member from different sources would be beneficial throughout the day.
Community Resources	We often provide our families with resources for things such as food banks, assistance with utility bills, and domestic violence hotlines. It would also be beneficial to include resources on social empowerment and leadership. Much of our work in the years to come will likely be helping students find their voice and giving them the ability to express it.
Student/Family Handouts on Trauma	It is important to ensure that students have the opportunity to learn about their own brains and their own trauma. Easy-access printouts for students that outline the biology of trauma, wellness, and mental health are good to give them for later reading or to discuss together.
Coloring Materials	Art is an important emotional outlet for people experiencing trauma at all ages, but especially for kids who have a difficult time expressing their emotions.
Journals/ Notebooks	Many students may move inward mentally as they process emotions. Sorting through these feelings takes time, and writing is a wonderful way to help students create an inner dialogue so they can better understand what they are experiencing.
Manipulatives	Stress balls, fidgets, and manipulative puzzles are essential for helping students slow their minds so they can begin to approach their emotions and express themselves. My all-time favorite is sand. Teachers have asked me to put my mini sandbox away during conferences because it is so addictive and soothing!
Information	Our students are smart. They are watching the world and they are talking to their friends about current events. They need adults who will answer their questions honestly and allow them the space to make their own informed decisions. We can help them evaluate sources and teach them how to seek out information to better equip their own ability to critically evaluate the world around them.

Informed Practices

Many of our families currently feel let down by the institutions that are supposed to be protecting their children—sometimes even including their schools. We must recognize with compassion that, rightfully so, parents need reassurance that we are a safe place for their children. Because of this, school staff could benefit from a little refresher on the do's and don'ts of thoughtful communication and classroom delivery. In chapter 1, we discussed calling home for rapport building; now let's dive a little deeper into how specific language can alter a conversation to be more open and productive.

Following COVID-19's emergence, conversations have taken on a much different shape. Moving forward, not only will we be potentially missing the in-person intimacy of conferences and pop-in visits, we should also be taking on conversations about topics such racism, stereotyping, and social advocacy. It will be especially important for all educators to honor their students and families by approaching these conversations with open listening skills and honesty. Staff members should take the time to educate themselves on these topics and may benefit from training to ensure everyone is comfortable allowing our families to express their concerns, feelings, and even doubts about the environment they are entrusting their children to.

Open and honest conversations can also occur in the classroom. Students benefit from voicing their concerns and feeling heard by others. Many of them also turn to their peers for support, and the classroom is a great space for them to do this with a guiding adult. To begin, curriculum should be evaluated to ensure that it is not only *un*biased but also supports *anti*-bias resources. The crisis team can help here too. Materials used in class must be critically evaluated to ensure that they are inclusive and unbiased. Crisis teams can work collaboratively with curriculum planning committees and help staff point out problematic areas that are biased and potentially retraumatizing to students.

> **We are reimagining what a class could look like when we remove outdated practices that may help only *some* students and adding more diverse activities that will benefit *all* students.**

This is where the fun part of reform comes in! Reducing material that could potentially retraumatize students does not mean leaving arbitrary holes in lesson planning. It means that we are reimagining what a class could look like when we remove outdated practices that may help only *some* students and adding more diverse activities that will benefit *all* students. By giving our students the green light to explore their feelings academically, we help them feel empowered as advocates rather than victims of unjust circumstances. Consider increasing some of the following activities and strategies to create lessons that encourage students to have a keen eye on justice and full grasp of the power of introspection:

- **Consider the source:** Evaluate primary and secondary sources in core content areas, then apply this to decision-making in the real world.

- **Growing philosophers:** Utilize strategies such as Socratic seminars to encourage students' abilities to express themselves, listen to others, and respectfully advocate for their views.

- **Inclusivity for the win!:** Use a wide range of inclusive materials as students learn, including diverse expert opinions, authors, and examples of culture within assignments, testing, and content.

- **A is for activism:** Teach students about activism and present the concept as a positive human trait in any core content area.

- **Read the room:** Show students that reading is a way to learn about the world, not just in a textbook but in informative texts (both nonfiction and fiction) that speak to everyone and every background.

- **Evaluating symbolism:** Take every opportunity to deep dive into symbolism and consumerism by showing children of all ages how to identify and criticize motive and propaganda using branding or messaging students are exposed to—even in traditional core content materials.

Chapter Summary

As students operate in fellowship, emotional responses to trauma spread like wildfire in schools. Trauma and crisis situations do not stop for school breaks or weekends. Our students are constantly experiencing stark changes and difficult times in their lives. Though educators typically return from summer refreshed and ready for a new year, sometimes each year gets more and more difficult for students. We have seen how this is magnified by larger arduous circumstances and traumas as well. Each new school year opens with students currently in crisis and in need of support—especially now, and for the foreseeable future. Our preventative committees have the power to bring together support for students, families, and staff in crisis situations. The crisis team is prepared to help teachers support students while respecting student privacy and anticipating possible retraumatization.

LOOKING AHEAD . . .

Next, we will expand on the importance of making sure supportive adults show students that they are there for them by being consistently present and available. Many of our students suffer from trauma without our knowledge, but ensuring that we have a clear and visible presence reminds them that we are here for them. Trauma can occur in the life of a single student at home (such as abuse or addiction in the family), in groups of students within a school (such as discrimination or a school shooting), and also on a larger scale within a city, where all students are experiencing the trauma at once (such as a hurricane or rioting). Building on what we have prepared for our rapport building, procedures, and crisis team, we will begin to evaluate how prepared our environment is for extensive responses.

CHAPTER 3

THE CITY: SIZEABLE TRAUMA

Examples of citywide trauma: destructive weather systems; mass shootings; police brutality; riots; compromised city resources (such as closed food banks, overcrowded hospitals, or contaminated water supplies); significant job losses; community drug use.

When traumatic things happen in our communities, towns, and cities. our sense of security is permanently changed. There is a difference between watching trauma on TV and experiencing it happen outside of our own window—or worse, being displaced because of the traumatic event. Our trauma responses are internalized and part of our daily lives, and the safety of hometown protection feels blotted out as we process what has happened.

For example, a friend of mine who lives in Minneapolis described her experience following the police murder of George Floyd as feeling "let down" by her city and city guardians. The trauma felt personal and deeply connected to her life because it happened within her own community.

We like to think that our students are safeguarded by the naivete of youth when there are traumatic events, but they see what is happening, they know how hurt people are, and they wonder if their family could be next. Sometimes, our students and their families are at the center of tragedy. This kind of fear is not only frightening in the moment, it is a long-lasting state of anxiety that children are waking to and walking in every day.

Having already helped school staff be mindful of the relationships they must build, and revamping crisis teams to support students in distress, the next step schools can take to update their trauma responses is taking a look at their local community. How can your town offer support for students? What kind of resources are present in your community? How do you know what assets will be helpful? What do you do when city infrastructures fail?

When there is trauma in the home, students can come to school to find the support they need to process their emotions. When trauma comes to or occurs in the school, the school can call on a team of crisis responders who can assist students and staff, while also using resources in the local community to reinforce security in the school. What do we do then when the city is traumatized?

The Perpetual Fallout from Community Stress

Citywide trauma alters the environment of thousands of people. When responses to a city's stress are lacking, the shortfalls can become normalized to citizens until they no longer try to resolve them. Hopelessness can lead people to simply "live with it" and suffer. Stress at this widespread level creates its own crisis for our students who depend on adults to make things better and help them heal.

My own city of Virginia Beach experienced a mass shooting in 2019, in which thirteen people were killed in one of our government municipal buildings. I had never experienced such a feeling of anguish watching it unfold and had not completely understood previously how worry and sadness could blanket an entire community. As we learned the details of the shooting, many of my educator friends came together in hopes of finding some sort of clarity for the return to school on Monday. What would we tell our students? How many of our students had personal relationships with the victims? Which students had parents who work for the city? What do we say when they ask us how this could have happened or why someone could be so violent? Indeed, when we walked through our doors to face our students, many of them had feelings they wanted to share, such as sadness from watching their parents' responses and anxiety over their parents' proximity to the shooting. Observations about how a family member could have easily been in the building processing a permit or other paperwork when the shooting occurred distracted the students for several weeks.

Citywide trauma alters the environment of thousands of people.

Over time, what we learned was that the trauma from the shooting was only part of the fear we and our students were feeling. There were many other layers of concern that were unearthed in that one horrific act. As stories of discontent in city offices were revealed, questions were asked about gun laws, fair treatment in the workplace, and the utility processing delays following the closing of the municipal center that caused housing and payment issues. It felt like our local safeguards were falling apart on many different levels. Stress from these subsidiary issues trickled down from adults to their children, working in tandem with our students' central fears over the violent act itself.

Ongoing protests and societal unrest have spread throughout our country and world to demand anti-racist policies and practices. I love that students are getting a front-row look at how citizens can take action and seek justice. Some students have also expressed some concern over the civil discord, specifically when it becomes violent and destructive. They wonder if people they love will be hurt, they wonder if their neighborhoods are safe places. And yet, there is also an internal conflict: how does one resolve one's fear of societal unrest while also shuddering to think of what life will be like if policy change does *not* take place and people do *not* end their racist behaviors? Our students are in desperate need of answers, and they need to

How does one resolve one's fear of societal unrest while also shuddering to think of what life will be like if policy change does *not* take place and people do *not* end their racist behaviors?

know who is there to help. They want to know what will happen next, and they have to be assured that we are right there with them, ready to put in the work to see change.

Action Items for Updating Response Procedures for Citywide Trauma

Trauma response at the city level requires knowing how to access community resources and digging deeper during times of change to find what else is available within the community. Typically, schools engage with community partners throughout the year to build stakeholder relationships and fortify the learning environment for students. Sometimes the school year begins in the midst of an emotional uphill battle, other times trauma hits suddenly and abruptly interrupts habitual comfort. City alliances may take different shapes to serve various circumstances.

Community partners are not only helpful in providing materials and services to schools, but also with helping students understand what is going on around them and what they can do to help locally. In this way, the schools and their surrounding city can assist each other in healing from a large traumatic situation. For example, a school might consider having hospital professionals speak at assemblies to discuss capacity issues and testing procedures, or directors of homeless shelters discuss the work they do in providing resources to people without housing. This not only educates children and helps schools answer difficult questions, it also provides an opportunity for the community partners to reach and inform large groups of citizens.

When we are knowledgeable about what our city has to offer our schools, we are better able to help support students when the city is in crisis. If certain infrastructures (housing services, motor services, Child Protective Services,

Figure 3.1 Action Items for Citywide Trauma

Protocol	Goal	Trauma Response Update Ideas
Community Resource Maps	*Create a visual of the "bigger picture" of city resources.*	• Use the crisis team to discuss possible needs based on recent trauma. • Contact community resources for guidance on local social service providers.
Community Contact Quick Sheet	*Have all resources with contact information in one place for quick reference.*	• Check to make sure your community resources support diverse needs. • Make paper copies for all teachers prior to beginning school.
Communication with Community Members	*Hold community conversations and locate support you might not know exists.*	• Reach out to community resources for consultations on support. • Schedule an open forum for community partners.
Student Contact Information	*Ensure access to all students even when they are not in the physical school.*	• Make contact lists available digitally so they can be accessed outside of school. • Provide hard copies for all crisis team members.

postal services, police departments, etc.) become fractured, we can lean on other resources in the city to help our students and families find safety and success. Perhaps more importantly, when our community partners are integrated within the school structure, students can learn to view their city as a working system. This might either help them regain a sense of security in their town or give them ideas of how to advocate for changes that are needed.

I think we all experienced times after our cities shut down because of the COVID-19 pandemic where we tried to call on some community office or service only to realize that they were not operational. Question after question came in from my students and families: from a student whose court date was the week after quarantine began, from an eighth grader who had questions about the Parks and Recreation program she was supposed to compete in, from a sixth grader who still needed volunteer hours for an honors program. I knew I could not fix all of the problems they were facing, and I had no one to reach out to for answers. Typically, if they had come to me while we were in school, I would have had easy access to people in the building and could have made quick calls to other offices. Instead, from my home computer, I had to parse out closures and work to find contact information for people within the community who could help them. By preparing a list of community contacts, making connections with people who work for local services, and having a sense of how city agencies operate together, you'll be better prepared to help your students when a crisis occurs.

Mapping the Community

In most of the schools I have been in, we did not have community maps in our trauma kits. We had community contact lists for services such as food banks, free glasses, clothing assistance, and so on, but until the pandemic hit the United States, we only pictured ourselves calling for help from within our schools, not from our temporary workspaces at home. Certain experts and resources were not within our reach, so we had to take more time figuring out how to access them. Working from a different environment led me to understand how a community map could bring a higher level of efficiency when trying to make heads or tails of what (and where) resources are available within the city. To prepare our crisis kits for the school years ahead, we can add community maps so our staff and crisis teams have access to a visual representation of where resources are located within the city.

By preparing a list of community contacts, making connections with people who work for local services, and having a sense of how city agencies operate together, you'll be better prepared to help your students when a crisis occurs.

A community map gives geographic locations and contact information for all of the different resources that organizations and non-profits within the city work hard to create so that when a citizen is in need, they can receive assistance. As I write this, the hurricane season is upon us in my coastal city, so pretend for a second that your city has been shut down by a damaging hurricane. A parent is in need of reduced-fee child care for your student who has not been completing his digital work and has a history of situational depression. The trauma team can look at the community map to find child care resources that are in areas that have been less affected by flooding or wind damage and more likely to have openings.

If resources on your map have closed or changed locations, the map still provides a starting point to show you who can help find the next solution that is still available. Updating the community map frequently prior to and during a city crisis will reflect the changing landscape of your city as it works through the situation. Communication with city officials, local news, and social media can play a vital role in managing the most recent updates. The goal is not to fix every problem our families might encounter, but rather to be able to point them in the right direction for possible solutions. The more informed we are about opportunities for assistance in our cities, the more resources we can give them. Some steps that might help a school create a community map are provided in figure 3.2.

Creating a community map may also be the perfect activity for your teachers as they participate in professional development before or during the school year.

It is important for all educators in your school to see the big picture of your city's resources so everyone can better understand where the city's strengths and weaknesses are. This activity can drive efforts within the school to fill in any gaps that the city doesn't provide (such as book and clothing drives), help with needs assessments, and help staff better understand the lives and struggles of their students' families. Need a good schoolwide project? Get students involved in researching and learning about their city and its services too!

Figure 3.2 Create a Community Map

	Step	Task
1	Review your contact sheet.	Look over established resources offered in the community and ensure that contact information is up-to-date. Make calls as necessary.
2	Hold a crisis team meeting.	Add additional contacts and brainstorm other resources that may be needed. Consider the current climate in your city.
3	Organize contacts and resources.	Map out geographic areas of your city and establish various counties or neighborhoods/school zones. Pinpoint places with services that might be useful to students or families.
4	Add the map to trauma procedures.	Ensure all members of the crisis team have a hard copy of and digital access to the community map.

Reaching Out to Your Community

With the community map completed, we can reach out to our community members to make sure they are ready to support our students. Unfortunately, with a depressed economy, we might have a lot of updating to do. Between closed businesses and households with less money and goods to donate, some of our usual resources may be stretched thin or no longer available.

We know the long-standing partners in our cities that we speak with on a regular basis throughout the school year. Those of us who were (or are still) supporting our students from home found that there were new challenges to helping in this context, and also realized that we had to be more integrated in the family system to aid students. We are used to being able to provide supports to create the optimal learning environment, but when the learning environment became the home, we had to broaden the scope of identifying barriers to education and who we pulled in from the community.

Even when your city is in need, there are some diamonds in the rough that you can dig up to provide your suffering students hope. For example, when you hear about the small non-profit organization that is handing out meals or the housing office that is working overtime to provide living spaces to families in need, you can be reassured that your city and its patrons are working together to help one another. This could be the key to bring renewed confidence and reassurance to your students experiencing trauma and help them heal.

The social unrest that students have been observing might also change the types of community resources we help them access. As systemic and institutional racism is laid bare, our students may wonder how their city feels about them. This might be terrifying to a student's sense of safety as they continue living in their city and attempt to participate in activities such as city-funded sports, playing in neighborhood parks, and shopping at local stores.

Schools must be able to distinguish themselves as leaders in anti-racism within their communities. Our BIPOC students experiencing continued stress and fear engaging in everyday activities likely struggle with a sense of apprehension approaching their schools and classrooms. As we use crisis protocols to establish school as a safe space, we need to attend to mending students' traumatized relationships with the larger community. Inviting community staples such as Urban Leagues and anti-racism coalitions will not only educate and unify students, but also provide a sense of agency to them.

As we use crisis protocols to establish school as a safe space, we need to attend to mending students' traumatized relationships with the larger community.

Figure 3.3 Identify Community Supports

Typical Community Supports: *Child Protective Services, parks and recreation departments, food banks, clothing donation organizations, volunteer vision services*	
New Supports and Possible Partnerships to Consider	
Wi-Fi providers	Help ensure that families have reliable, affordable Wi-Fi in their homes to facilitate digital instruction.
Medical caregivers	Bring medical professionals from the community into the school to teach students about safety precautions.
Phone-in translation services	Use translation services to check in on your English language learning families and provide any resources needed.
Urban League	Ask speakers to come into the school to teach students about advocacy and opportunities to interact with government officials.
Cultural centers	Ask speakers to come in to teach students about the diverse cultures that live in their own community and inform students of opportunities to participate in various cultural causes.

Sharing Resources with Students

Having reached out to some of the resources your community has to offer your students and their families, the next question is, how will you get that information to them? The obvious answer is connecting with them at school, of course. But we have learned that our trauma protocols have to be prepared to respond to even the most shocking scenarios that might happen . . . like a global pandemic.

It really is amazing to think about all of the ways the school network communicates throughout a regular school day to reach students and gain information. When I need information from or about a student, I typically do not email teachers, because they are busy conducting a classroom. Instead, I might drop into classrooms, walk the hallways, pop into a grade-level or content staff meeting, leave a note in a mailbox, or send a pass to a homeroom class. These actions come as second nature to me, and I didn't realize how much I leaned on them for my counseling practice until they were no longer available to me.

When we first closed down, my school administration learned that without quick access to teachers in person, we needed to have a digital space that had all communication regarding students in one place. I struggled to find the right medium when I wanted to reach out to a large group of kids or when parents notified me about a student crisis, because emails take so long to coordinate efforts.

After about a week we started to construct our digital schools. I set up a group space on Schoology (the online educational program we were already using in the brick-and-mortar classroom) and our school used a Google Doc for the entire student body. At a 370-student caseload and 1,600-student school population, this was quite a task! It was one of the most inspiring team efforts of educators I have ever seen.

Moving forward, we would be remiss if we did not learn from this experience. Trauma preparedness might benefit from the following digital changes:

- Survey students to inquire about their internet access at home, including what types of devices they have access to and what their Wi-Fi accessibility is.

  > Provide technical workshops and assistance to parents so they can feel confident supporting their students from home on any number of devices (including smartphones).

- Have students enroll in or sign up for online platforms, even if they will not be used regularly during the school year. All staff should send the same message to students regarding digital access to their classrooms and crisis team members (such as school counselors and social workers).

> Ensure students have time to practice on this platform throughout the school year and make it clear that they understand that this is where everyone will meet should we move to digital instruction again.

- Create a spreadsheet with student information connected to a reliable online service so all staff members can access it from inside or outside the school.

> Decide on the information you would like to have on the spreadsheet and follow district directives on how or where this can be done confidentially. For example, I pulled data on parent occupations and added that as a tab on the spreadsheet so that teachers had quick access to this information.

My own school counseling team created a digital page for each of our caseloads. Within our student group pages, we were able to schedule individual, group, and lunch bunch sessions with students and also allow them to have a social space to communicate with each other. This gave us immeasurable data on how students were feeling and faring during the school closure. On the spreadsheet that the whole staff could access, we collected information so that if a teacher noticed a student was not performing academically, they could quickly see whether other teachers have been able to reach the parents, what the parents' occupations and availability are, and how the student is performing in other classes.

In the years to come, I hope to see these efforts as an additional part of our trauma preparedness for our school annually. Consider this scenario for the importance of easy communication systems that anticipate a large-scale crisis:

Mr. Grande notices that Steven has abruptly stopped completing his digital work. He tries to call home but has not heard back from the parent. He accesses the All-Student Spreadsheet and sees that Steven has stopped completing work in all classes and notices that one teacher mentioned that upon speaking with his mom, she said she was overwhelmed with the at-home education as a single mom juggling two students and work.

Mr. Grande alerts his administrators, who have not been able to reach the parent on the phone either but begin to prepare hard-copy work for the student to complete in the event that he has relocated or is having difficulty with internet access.

Mr. Grande checks the parent occupation tab, sees that Steven's mom is a nurse, and realizes she is likely working overtime, as the local hospital is over capacity, and it is therefore possible Steven has been cared for in someone else's home. He reaches out to the school counselor, who reports that Steven has still been attending Lunch Bunch Zoom meetings but has not mentioned any difficulties. She is able to check in with him there.

Steven says that he is staying at his grandparent's house for most of the week, so he is feeling down and missing his mom. The counselor and Mr. Grande are able to consult and create a plan for Steven to be able to catch up on the work, the administrators deliver hard-copy packets of work, and the teacher gets Steven's cell phone number to schedule weekly phone calls to check in.

Chapter Summary

For many school staff, it feels like the educational system has flipped upside down and dropped us on our heads. As we have figured out how to amend our current practices, however, we have realized just how strong we are and how impactful we can be to students. We have the potential to be the safe place and the glue that tethers students to their place in the city. When there are trauma-inducing situations, the schools should be able to find resources within the community for students. When this occurs, the schools become an anchor for students even when they feel like their city is broken.

LOOKING AHEAD . . .

We have discussed how important training and communication will be at school in the coming months and years. Our students have experienced crisis in the home, the school, and the city at this point. Who would have ever thought that our whole world might be impacted by such large-scale traumas as what we have seen? The last review needed for our crisis teams and trauma protocols involved the ways in which we approach students following mass-scale trauma, as we've all experienced with the COVID-19 pandemic. Gone are the days when we rely on gradual team building and take our time to establish connections with students and families. As our students enter their schools from now on, they will all have experienced recent global trauma and will need us to be more present and supportive than ever.

CHAPTER 4

THE STATE/COUNTRY/WORLD: MASS-SCALE TRAUMA

Examples of mass-scale trauma: economic depression; acts of terrorism; pandemics; institutional racism; societal discontent; acts of war; widespread weather events.

Some time ago, this section may have started with something like, "How do we even conceptualize trauma that is so big that an entire world experiences stress simultaneously?" Lo and behold, the infamous Year 2020 taught us what global trauma looks like. When reports of a fast-spreading virus began to seep into one country after another, the whole world sat and watched the news in disbelief. What we have found is that the key to surviving and thriving in a global crisis is connection. Families held group phone chats, book clubs met online, teachers made YouTube videos, friends connected on social media, and we embraced (or attempted to embrace) the virtual school environment.

Educators in different cities, states, and countries found each other through digital groups and roundtables. The glue that held us together was realizing that we were all experiencing many of the same struggles both personally and professionally. We compared local scenarios, asked questions, brainstormed, and inspired each other. This socialization and comradery brought us all together, and then we worked individually to develop our own practices. I cannot even begin to describe how much my school's virtual staff meetings and counseling department meetings carried me through the year, professionally and personally.

While educators reimagined their new digital world, our students' development was also being altered. When an individual student experiences an individual or small-group trauma, we have to envelop and protect them. On the other hand, when they are part of a massive-scale traumatic experience, our availability and presence have to be in overdrive for all our students. We already have a general awareness of the crisis they are experiencing. With this vulnerability exposed, we want to draw the students in with shared discussions and then process each student's personal experience privately.

I can remember being in the car a day or two after 9/11. While I stopped at a traffic light, surrounded by several cars, a jet flew overhead. For context, my city is home to several different military bases of various branches. "Jet noise" is a common term because in the majority of the city you can hear large and fast aircraft overhead. But at this time, we were all still shocked from the international tragedy and airspace was heavily restricted. As I sat and stared at the jet, the light changed, and I didn't even notice. No other driver honked their horn, and I looked around to see people in their cars sitting and watching as well. As we started to wake from our trances, everyone quietly glanced at each other with question in their eyes. We were strangers with the same concern, and when the light changed for the second time, we knew that we were all worried that the jet was another terrorist attack. I will never forget this feeling of such shared, large-scale emotion with people I have never met and will never see again. Our students, their families, and we—their counselors and teachers—are going through this type of event now. We are all here together.

We want to draw the students in with shared discussions and then process each student's personal experience privately.

Tailoring Comprehensive Trauma Interventions for Individual Students

Considering that our students may be experiencing trauma in layers ranging from individual homelife to worldwide health crisis, we will also see varied social and emotional responses. Built into schedules, consistent and comprehensive programs that foster social and emotional health will reach all students. With each additional crisis, trauma recovery plans can also be tailored to each student. Let's take a look at a student who has experienced extensive trauma in many different spheres of their life.

> **Devin is a fifth-grade student with a history of truancy for the majority of her education. Her mom communicates well with the schools, but she does not have alternate transportation from the city bus and often oversleeps because she works the night shift at a skilled nursing facility. Devin knows that if she misses the bus, there will be no one to get her to school. They also need help with the child care of younger children at home. Mom is always open to receiving help from the school and has let the counselor know that she got her GED instead of finishing high school, and so does not always feel confident being an authority with Devin's schooling.**

When the COVID-19 pandemic hit, mom's already stretched funds also took a hit. While the school was still open, she reduced her shift in the nursing facility out of fear of exposing Devin and her classmates to the virus. After schools shut down, she had to make up for the lost wages by working extra shifts, and Devin was often at home alone with her younger siblings. Now, Devin has found out she may need to travel to another state with her mom because her grandmother is in the hospital with COVID-19, and her grandfather needs help with day-to-day activities. Devin continues to be behind with work, feels responsible for her mom and siblings' safety, and is worried about her grandparents surviving the virus.

Figure 4.1 Sample Individualized Intervention for Mass-Scale Trauma

- Individual counseling meetings
- Connect with mom
- Assess needs in home

- Connect with school social worker
- Collaborate with teachers on classroom support
- Establish plan for supplemental meetings

Family health concerns; Lack of structure in the home due to old/new financial stress (self/home)

Loss of teacher and peer interaction due to COVID-19 school closures (school)

Feelings of fear and hopelessness caused by turbulence on the news (country)

Stressed community resources, such as child care for siblings (city)

- Classroom mindfulness practice
- Embedded critical thinking skills
- Easy access to crisis team

- Create community partner mentorship
- Provide mom with community resources
- Research neighborhood needs

Figure 4.1 shows what an individualized program might look like for a student like Devin. Devin's education was already in jeopardy with at-risk factors from before the school closures. Interventions for the country-wide trauma can be built into the school environment, physical or virtual, for all students, with additional personalized interventions for trauma on smaller scales. Because Devin has trauma in the home, each tier is magnified, making comprehensive support even more essential.

Action Items for Updating Response Procedures for Mass-Scale Trauma

We know that upon returning from a national or international crisis we will walk into a school full of students who have been exposed to some level of trauma over the course of the event. Actually, let's try that again. We know that we will *connect* in *some way* (digitally or in person) with a school full of students who have experienced some level of trauma at some point. The mere fact that our students spent an entire summer not knowing if they would physically be able to walk their school hallways in the fall is traumatic.

Where do we start in determining what support students will need from us following a major crisis? Based on what students have asked for with citywide trauma, our presence will be the biggest benefit to their emotional well-being. They will need us to be there, to bridge the gap between the new way of life and the old way of life. They will need us to bring them consistency and boundaries. They will need us to bring some semblance of peace to their chaotic world.

Planning to simply exist and interact with students may seem inconsequential because of the constant state of crisis our world and country have been in during recent months. However, we can provide a safe space that shows students that through all of the catastrophes, education is still firmly in place to be there for them and help them through life. This message is going to propel the students into a world where they can once again feel solid footing in life and within their communities. We have to tell them, "We are here for you, with whatever you need."

We can provide a safe space that shows students that through all of the catastrophes, education is still firmly in place to be there for them and help them through life.

Preparation for trauma response can be ongoing, with many opportunities throughout the school year to train staff and roll out schoolwide initiatives. Though the crisis team defines specific goals and tasks, professional development workshops can include all staff in brainstorming and deciding how best to embed and disperse information on trauma. Allowing staff the opportunity to play a part in schoolwide SEL programs also increases the likelihood of buy-in from all staff members, which will create a more robust program. Some of these structures might already be in place, such as the PBIS program we use in my school. We

Figure 4.2 Action Items for Mass-Scale Trauma

Protocol	Goal	Trauma Response Update Ideas
Establish Educator Presence with Students	*Assure established modes of communication with students for SEL support.*	• Increase modes of communication for SEL opportunities. • Brainstorm opportunities with teachers for connecting digitally with students.
Prepare Emergency Materials to Access at Home	*Staff are prepared to have everything needed for a successful digital office at home.*	• All staff should set up their "go-to" binders. • Assess office materials so all staff have quick access to an at-home office kit, virtual and/or physical.
Collect SEL and mindfulness resources	*Ensure resources are ready to help give students tools for stress release.*	• Create a list of easy mindfulness activities for the classroom or individual students. • Allocate time in schedule for SEL lessons.
Design SEL/ Mindfulness Curriculum	*Evaluate curriculum to ensure it is inclusive, anti-racist, and all-encompassing.*	• Provide guidelines for content preparation meetings to evaluate the inclusivity of lessons. • Ensure current events are part of the curriculum as well as opportunities for student expression.

already have the vessel; we just need to add to it! Other schoolwide interventions, such as one-minute meditation breaks or daily positive quotes in each hallway, might quickly become part of your school culture with full staff on board.

We now know that we also need to be ready to move our SEL practices online at a moment's notice. In doing so, we will be able to continue supporting our students even if it is from home. This kind of consistency will also bridge students' worlds between the old way of life to the new unpredictable reality.

The Importance of Educators' Presence

A clear educator presence in the brick-and-mortar school includes extra presence in the hallways, intentional time spent connecting in various classrooms, and schoolwide campaigns using inspirational phrasing and messaging. We will hopefully get the chance to do this in each school year to come, but if not, we can still provide our students with plenty of support. Even digitally, we can make sure students know we are there for them. This can help them feel safe and confident enough to begin to return to normal activities.

When a student enters the school with trepidation and finds staff members in place and ready to fully engage with them, they receive the message that no matter what happens, we will still be there to help. When we are online again in the years to come—and we very likely will be—we can take steps to make sure that we are prepared to surround the student similarly, even if it is through technology.

When students experience trauma, they may lose faith in securities or beliefs they have trusted in, so the best thing we can do to regain their confidence is to show them that we are their protection. In my school, for example, as a counselor I do not have a specified "digital room" set up automatically (like a teacher who has assigned sections) on our instructional platform online. Because of this, I have to make sure I am aware of all the steps teachers are taking to instruct students online. This is not for my own practice per se, but for my ability to embed with the teachers. In doing so I am able to join them in their classrooms and give the students the illusion that I am "popping in" the way I would on the hallway.

Many of my teacher colleagues have made similar changes. While they would typically greet each student at their classroom door and stop into the cafeteria to chat with students, they were instead developing check-in practices in the mornings to reach students (through their digital classroom, emails, or social media) and developing lunch bunch office hours online. Teachers and staff can prepare by ensuring we have an A, B, and C plan for connecting with students and providing social and emotional learning. Consider the example in figure 4.3 of a schoolwide program that is ready to anticipate any circumstance that may arise, including in-person, digital, and mixed deliveries.

Some of the activities on page 51 were already established in most schools prior to the year 2020 or were quickly established once instruction moved online across the country. Now that we live in a world where these scenarios are plausible at a moment's notice, it is important for us to firm up our planning. By making a similar table, you can fill in your Plan A and Plan B with new and established schoolwide interventions and add an altered plan (Plan C) with specific instructions so that teachers have a guide to help them transition to online instruction, if necessary.

Preparedness for a Quick Move

Though most educators came into this field to work with children and help teach them up to adulthood, many of us also share a secondary passion: office supplies. We are overzealous about those things that will organize our chaotic classrooms and offices. The ergonomic mouse and mousepad, folders, tapes, labels, and beautifully constructed binders or online organizational apps become our comrades and allies as we muscle through the day with hundreds of children.

Figure 4.3 Sample Schoolwide Plans for Various Circumstances

Plan A In School		
Programs	Planning Needs	Delivery
• Mindful Moments at the end and beginning of the school day • Check-ins/check-outs for students in trauma • SEL lessons in content classes • Staff supports with open-door office policy • Social opportunities like lunch bunches, groups, after-school activities, etc.	✔ Include mindfulness in morning announcements ✔ Alter Master Schedule as needed for check-ins/outs ✔ Distribute SEL lessons to teachers ✔ Clarify and post crisis team members and locations ✔ Clarify and post social opportunities in hallways, classrooms, and announcements	Classrooms, hallways, lunchrooms

Plan B All Online		
Programs	Planning Needs	Delivery
• Mindful Moments distributed through emails daily • Check-in online office hours • SEL lesson videos for whole-school use • Staff office hours posted clearly and sent home often • Virtual lunch bunches, virtual field trips with live discussion thread, movie night with live discussion thread, etc. • Send postcards to students with encouragement	✔ Coordinate consistent schoolwide use of tools for lessons and messages ✔ Clarify and post crisis team availability and access ✔ Have a central location for social events ✔ Ensure consistent and schoolwide parameters for content classrooms ✔ Divide student body among all staff for mailings and check-in phone calls, if needed	Online platform, YouTube, email

Plan C Moving Online During the Year		
Programs	Planning Needs	Delivery
• Keep pacing between Plan A and Plan B for seamless transition • Identify what parts of each plan can be used for mixed instruction of both in-person and online environments	✔ Both Plans A and B should be completed and established prior to school opening ✔ Establish beforehand how long it should take for teachers to move to the digital plan following an abrupt closure	Have an established and central mode of communication for staff prior to closure

These supplies will also serve a purpose in our preparations to respond to children (and adults) in crisis.

When I have a practicum or internship student, the first thing I tell them is to set up their master information binder. I call this binder my "bible," adopted from my own internship experience in which I was advised to do the same. This binder is my go-to resource in the school because I can bring it to any meeting and provide information to support a staff member, student, or family member with accessible ease. It is also the first thing I pick up to bring home when there is a possible school closure due to a weather event or, as it turns out, a pandemic. Some people prefer this to be digital, such as a flash drive or cloud storage space. The purpose of both in-hand and online tools is the same: to have a central location that holds all the information needed to access students and all the complex details that make a school operate. My binder is filled with the following information.

Figure 4.4 Sample Contents of a Master Information Binder

Tab	Contents	Useful for ...
Calendars	district calendar, activities calendar, testing calendar	planning and organization
Master Schedule	all school, class, and staff schedules	schedule changes from home, identifying classes
Caseload	all student lists including my caseload, student schedules, rosters, focus groups, 504, IEP, ESL, etc.	easy access to all students and their information
School Information	facility use, bus lists, phone instructions, testing result parameters for class placement	quick referencing for planning, use with student/parent questions
Resources	community resources, city municipal contact information, military liaison officers, master copies of handouts	information to give to families for support, increase community partnership
Trauma Response	Crisis Team list, trauma response protocol	easy access in times of crisis or intervention planning

In addition to having our main informational binder or digital file, we might also want to prepare an emergency kit to take home if necessary during a catastrophic crisis that impedes the learning environment. This might include extra folders, notes, copy paper, and information such as 504 and intervention binders.

With backup plans in place and access to thorough supplies, we can be equipped to set up our educational practices from anywhere.

Intentional Practices: Teaching SEL and Mindfulness

When students are exposed to trauma, their minds and hearts are stormed by negative and fearful emotions. As discussed in the individual trauma section, the long-term effects of constant stress and fight-or-flight panic response can cause a number of reactions in a student. We can aid an entire student body by putting practices into place that teach them (and the staff) how to better cope with constant stress and uncertainty.

As we set up our schools to receive students, we want to think of ways that we can reach those students who have experienced trauma through large-scale events. SEL provides students with skills that will help them continue learning and engaging even when they are experiencing stressful situations. This includes honest and direct anti-racism content that builds on humanitarianism and global thinking to address historic and systemic racism and other institutional inequities. Schools must also be prepared to respond to educators who are resistant to delivering these types of lessons to ensure that all staff are not only trained in this area but cognitively aware that racism is a threat to our students and society. We would be gravely mistaken to omit this type of learning—for both students and educators—and should make it a priority to build time into our schedules to ensure students are receiving this developmental learning.

SEL lessons are perfect as embedded information within standard content areas. The best-case scenario is that the entire staff are trained and have been given materials or similar strategies. In this way, students will internalize the strategies by hearing the same thing from multiple staff members. Once healthy coping strategies become part of the school culture, students can begin to control their own emotions, and mental well-being practices will be instilled. Many schools and districts already have programs such as Responsive Classroom, Second Step, CASEL, Rethink SEL, and the like. During a time of crisis, however, it is important that these efforts be stepped up and leaned on by reinforcing the lessons throughout the day and in every corner of the school.

When students are better able to calm their own emotions, they will also be able to focus better and learn more efficiently. Mindfulness practices can do this for our students—and build in the opportunity for teachers to get a conscious

Once healthy coping strategies become part of the school culture, students can begin to control their own emotions, and mental well-being practices will be instilled.

breather during stressful times as well! Here are some quick ways that mindfulness training can be taught to students for healthier emotional responses and better focus on the learning materials:

- **Learn and practice breathing techniques such as 4x4 or box breathing.** Start each class with deep breathing privately at each desk.

- **Develop skills that lead to calming meditation practice.** Have brain breaks in the middle of each class that begin at 10 seconds and slowly increase to 30–60 seconds.

- **Create gratitude journals or cards in each English class.** Allow time for students to reflect on positive and comforting things in their lives.

- **Use quiet natural observations in science class.** Start labs and experiments with 15–30 seconds of quiet observation of materials to help students learn focusing skills and engage personally with the materials.

- **Allow student voice projects in social studies.** Help students feel agency over their place in the world by teaching them how to speak about, and advocate for, injustice.

- **Utilize meditative counting for 10–20 seconds in math classes.** Have students use meditative skills with numbers (counting, tracing formulas with fingers, repetitive counting) to help them focus and make the math room a soothing place to be.

Though we wish we could, we cannot take away the painful situations that some of our students are in. We can, however, empower them to gain confidence in their mental and emotional capacities even in times of trauma. Mindfulness allows students to observe their emotions before moving forward and to process them instead of hiding them away inside to fester. When speaking with students during this time, I typically revert to an old Play Therapy class from grad school in which my professor told us that by allowing our clients to feel their emotions, we are telling them that every part of them is accepted and valuable. Simply responding to their expressions with observations (such as, "You are angry. You wish this were different. You feel unheard.") allows students to own their feelings before beginning to tackle them.

Chapter Summary

I anticipate that much of our trauma work in the years to come will occur as issues from the recent national and global traumas begin to be uncovered.

Students may arrive to school (or their digital platform) with a smile, but will likely peel layers back to expose their experience with trauma over the course of weeks or months. By providing schoolwide programs to all students, we will be one step ahead of the game. As signifying behaviors begin to emerge (see examples in chapter 1), we can add interventions to match. We will have to be proactive and patient. We will need to all work together. We have our work cut out for us.

LOOKING AHEAD . . .

As educators, we are communicators and thinkers. Now that we have done all this thinking about how to set up the school to respond to students in crisis, it is time to get to work! Creating a Trauma Response Worksheet (page 60) and a Quick Sheet (page 58) for staff will help us be prepared to put all of our plans in motions and fully support our students when they return to school, however that may look. I wish you well in this work, which is difficult yet so important. And I'd love to hear about your successes—and your struggles. Please feel free to reach me through my publisher: help4kids@freespirit.com or visit my website: weekendtherapy.wordpress.com.

SPOTLIGHT . . .

Supporting Military-Connected Students

I would betray my sprawling military hometown if I did not include specific supports that our military-connected students could benefit from. I asked my friend and colleague Amanda Yoder, a military-connected school counselor, to give insight into this group of students who never cease to amaze me with their sacrifice, resilience, and confidence.

While COVID-19 and recent anti-racism protests and riots have presented challenges for all students, students who have a parent in the military faced some additional challenges. On March 16, 2020, the Department of Defense issued a stop order for almost all military travel, including over 3 million active duty, reservists, and DOD civilians. Military-connected families who were in the middle of a move or about to move found themselves halted unexpectedly. They were stationed around the world, cut off from family and without many of their belongings that had already been shipped away. Students who had a loved one deployed saw deployments extended for an unknown period of time or had a parent on a ship unable to pull into port (which may be the only time they can connect by phone). Even now as many places begin to reopen, military members are restricted from many activities such as eating out and traveling.

Another military-connected group of students impacted very differently by recent events are National Guard families. National Guard members are not typically located in large military areas and often work normal civilian jobs most of the time. Recently they have been activated in large numbers to assist with COVID-19 relief efforts–from distributing PPE to hospitals to assisting with nursing home testing. Some Guard members were used to supplement local law enforcement as anti-racism protests swept the nation. These Guard members and their families have had to have difficult conversations about their new role, as it is quite different from the typical disaster assistance role that National Guard are primarily trained for. In both instances, Guard families are worried about their loved ones' safety, and they rarely have the support systems that active duty members do.

How can you best support these students? One military student may struggle with a deployed parent, another with moving, and another with living with a grandparent due to a deployment. It is important to learn more about the impact of a mass-scale trauma like the pandemic on your local military families. It will be different depending if they are active duty, National Guard, or other branch of service (Air Force, Army, Navy, Marine Corps, or Coast Guard). Be mindful that these students are, naturally, a full cross-section of your school: they include all races, ethnicities, genders, sexual orientations, and socio-economic statuses.

Here are some resources that can be used to support military students:

- Military One Source (MilitaryOneSource.mil) provides telehealth, mental health support, financial counseling, and other resources.

- Tutor.com/military offers free tutoring by voice or chat to assist military students on assignments and various subjects.

- Families Overcoming Under Stress, Military Kids Connect, Military Child Education Coalition, Operation Homefront, Blue Star Families, and the USO all offer various support services for military-connected students and their families.

- Individual military branch readiness and support centers will have advice specific to their branch.

TEACHER QUICK SHEET FOR TRAUMA RESPONSE

Observe Students Report non-emergency signs of stress to: _____	Obvious Signs of Trauma and Stress	Less Obvious Signs of Trauma and Stress
	• Swift drop in grades • Despondency • Detachment from peers • Sleepiness or lethargy • Abrupt attendance change • Skipping meals • Mood changes/emotional outbursts	• Lingering around the counselor's office • Less interest in hobbies • Bouts of daydreaming • Increased requests to call home • Loitering in the bathrooms • Increased obsession with order • Constant questioning/ double-checking

Call Home	• Begin with a general check-in with the parent.
	
	  › Express concern.
	
	• Discuss something you love about their child.
	
	  › Personalize your knowledge of the student.
	
	• Check in with your own feelings as you discuss the behavior in question.
	
	  › Generalize problem behaviors in the classroom.
	
	• Let the parent know you are concerned and why.
	
	  › Avoid "why" questions; use "we" instead of "he/she/you."
	
	• Listen.
	
	  › Do not interpret their frustration as criticism.
	
	• Ask the parent how they feel.
	
	  › Sense when a parent is overwhelmed and note sources of stress in the home.
	
	• Make a plan that includes solicited advice from the parent.
	
	  › Take the weight off of their shoulders and refer them to specialists.	

Reach Out	Crisis Team Member Name and Contact Information
Child Protective Services Hotline #: _____	1.
Non-Emergency #: _____	2.
	3.
	4.
	5.

Prepare Materials	Materials Provided from School	Materials for Trauma Kit
	Trauma procedures	Master information binder or digital file
	Community resources and map	Stress relief manipulatives
	Master copies of trauma handouts	Notebooks and coloring materials
	Drafts of emergency correspondence scripts	Office supplies ready to go

Teach Mindfulness	
	• Check-ins/check-outs with students
	• Lunch bunches and other social opportunities
	• Reserved time for student discussion on current events
	• 4x4/box breathing practice
	• Meditative quiet brain breaks (can use soft sounds in the background)
	• Gratitude reflections
	• Observe nature and environmental sounds/sights
	• Projects centered on advocacy
	• Repetitive counting for relaxation
	• Tactile tracing of hand, desk, or provided designs

TRAUMA RESPONSE PREPARATIONS WORKSHEET FOR SCHOOL PLANNING

Professional Development *(check choices)*

✔	Topic	Date	Lead Facilitators
	Signs of Trauma		
	Positive/Productive Communication		
	Trauma Response Review		
	Crisis Team Functions		
	Digital Connection Plan		
	SEL/Mindfulness Lessons		

Trauma Protocol

Local emergency contacts and phone numbers	
Parent contact expectations for staff	
Staff and administration to be notified	
Location of staff parent contact documentation	
Location of staff intervention plan documentation	

Emergency Statement Blueprints *(check when complete, circle topic)*

✔	Message Avenue	Location Saved	Topic
	Email		Weather/Violence/Medical/Discrimination/Other:
	Phone		Weather/Violence/Medical/Discrimination/Other:
	Letter		Weather/Violence/Medical/Discrimination/Other:

Crisis Team Planning

Crisis team members:

Crisis team schedule:

Crisis team roles and school/district protocols:

Community map workshop date and goals:

☐ Review community resources list

☐ Workshop with crisis team

☐ Organize contacts and resources geographically

Interventions and SEL/Mindfulness Plan

Programs	Plan A Current (or Additional) In-Person SEL/Mindfulness Programs	Plan B Digital Variations
Planning Needs		
Delivery System		
Plan C Parameters for Moving Online During the Year		

ACTION ITEMS AT-A-GLANCE

Self/Home-Based Trauma

Protocol	Goal	Trauma Response Update Ideas
Calling Home	Ensure there is a protocol for calling home for trauma inquiries.	• Provide professional development (PD) on family communication. • Use specific activities to teach the protocol in PD groups.
Relationship Building	Allow time for building relationships with students throughout the day.	• Evaluate staff schedules to allow time for relationship building. • Create mentorships, check-ins/outs, and/or advisory programs.
Emergency Numbers	Emphasize mandated reporting requirements and ensure all staff have community emergency numbers.	• Provide handouts to post in each classroom. • Include the information in PD.
School Trauma Response	Establish a schoolwide trauma response protocol and make sure staff are up-to-date.	• Provide a copy to each teacher for the classroom and include it in all substitute teacher folders. • Construct PD workshops using sample scenarios.
Needs Assessments	Create assessments and collect data to find out what your students need.	• Determine the assessment's purpose and create assessments within PD groups. • Use assessment data in PD workshops to address student needs.

School-Based Trauma

Protocol	Goal	Trauma Response Update Ideas
Crisis Team	Establish or bolster a crisis team and create a team meeting schedule.	• Distribute to staff a list of crisis team members. • Schedule crisis team meetings and send invitations.
Trauma Kit	Create a trauma kit to use in crisis situations that will aid in supporting students and families (see figure 2.3 on page 30 for items to include).	• Research and add specific information about safety and wellness. • Research and add honest information about systemic racism and advocacy.
Statement Blueprints	Prepare statements/scripts for emails, letters, and phone calls home to use in possible crisis situations.	• Ensure the crisis team has input in and access to statements. • Provide teachers with statements for reference.
Scripts for Teachers	Help teachers practice talking with parents about trauma.	• Provide hard copy quick sheets to teachers. • Hold PD workshops with sample scenarios.

Citywide Trauma		
Protocol	Goal	Trauma Response Update Ideas
Community Resource Maps	Create a visual of the "bigger picture" of city resources.	• Use the crisis team to discuss possible needs based on recent trauma. • Contact community resources for guidance on local social service providers.
Community Contact Quick Sheet	Have all resources with contact information in one place for quick reference.	• Check to make sure your community resources support diverse needs. • Make paper copies for all teachers prior to beginning school.
Communication with Community Members	Hold community conversations and locate support you might not know exists.	• Reach out to community resources for consultations on support. • Schedule an open forum for community partners.
Student Contact Information	Ensure access to all students even when they are not in the physical school.	• Make contact lists available digitally so they can be accessed outside of school. • Provide hard copies for all crisis team members.
Mass-Scale Trauma		
Protocol	Goal	Trauma Response Update Ideas
Establish Educator Presence with Students	Assure established modes of communication with students for SEL support.	• Increase modes of communication for SEL opportunities. • Brainstorm opportunities with teachers for connecting digitally with students.
Prepare Emergency Materials to Access at Home	Staff are prepared to have everything needed for a successful digital office at home.	• All staff should set up their "go-to" binder. • Assess office materials so all staff have quick access to an at-home office kit, virtual and/or physical.
Collect SEL and Mindfulness Resources	Ensure resources are ready to give students tools for stress release.	• Create a list of easy mindfulness activities for the classroom or individual students. • Allocate time in schedule for SEL lessons.
Design SEL/ Mindfulness Curriculum	Evaluate curriculum to ensure it is inclusive, anti-racist, and all-encompassing.	• Provide guidelines for your content preparation meetings to evaluate the inclusivity of lessons. • Ensure current events are part of the curriculum as well as opportunities for student expression.

RECOMMENDED RESOURCES

Anti-Bias and Equity

A Framework for Understanding Poverty by Ruby K. Payne, Ph.D. (aha! Process Inc., 2005). A non-fiction work outlining the struggles and barriers of poverty and class in the United States.

Reviving Ophelia: Saving the Selves of Adolescent Girls by Mary Pipher, Ph.D., and Sara Pipher Gilliam (Riverhead, 2005). A non-fiction work that beautifully describes gendered difficulties many pre-teen and teen girls face as they come of age and provides strategies for raising independent and strong women.

EduColor. educolor.org. A conglomerate group of professionals passionate about ensuring equality and fairness for BIPOC students in schools. Also check out executive director José Luis Vilson's website for amazing videos and inspiration: thejosevilson.com.

GLSEN. glsen.org. A comprehensive resource for advocacy for LGBTQ students, including groups, clubs, and lessons.

Teaching Tolerance. tolerance.org. An organization founded by the Southern Poverty Law Center dedicated to human rights and the educational environment, including classroom lessons, free publications, and many more resources.

Classroom Planning

Champ for Kids by Kelly Hoggard (EduGladiators, 2019). An inspiring non-fiction book on advocacy in educators of all ages, accompanied by a thoughtful and active weekly Twitter Chat #champforkids.

The Curious Classroom by Harvey "Smokey" Daniels (Heineman, 2017). An educator's perspective on engaging students through our own curiosities.

Crisis Teams

Middle School Moment (PBS FRONTLINE, 2012). pbs.org/video/frontline -middle-school-moment. This video series and accompanying school program focuses on the work of a crisis team in an inner-city middle school, but it could inspire any grade level's program.

Intervention Central. interventioncentral.org. A go-to resource for all things behavior and academic intervention, including tools to generate checklists, grade scales, or rewards systems.

Motivational Interviewing Skills

"17 Motivational Interviewing Questions and Skills" (Positive Psychology, 2020). positivepsychology.com/motivational-interviewing. A comprehensive list and explanation of the use of "motivational interviewing skills" as we communicate with others.

"A Summary of Eight Counseling Microskills" (Australian Institute of Professional Counsellors, 2012). counsellingconnection.com/index.php/2012/08/09 /counselling-micro-skills-a-summary. A great description of the "interviewing skills" school counselors employ to practice patience and communication with students and families.

Trauma and SEL

Mindful Classrooms: Daily 5-Minute Practices to Support Social-Emotional Learning (PreK to Grade 5), by James Butler, M.Ed. (Free Spirit, 2019). A guide for busy elementary educators on how to easily incorporate mindfulness activities into existing curriculum.

The PBIS Team Handbook: Setting Expectations and Building Positive Behavior, by Char Ryan, Ph.D., and Beth Baker, M.S.Ed. (Free Spirit, 2019). This handbook provides detailed guidelines for implementing and sustaining PBIS for schools and teams.

The SEL Solution: Integrate Social and Emotional Learning into Your Curriculum and Build a Caring Climate for All by Jonathan C. Erwin, M.A. (Free Spirit, 2019). Inspiring and practical guide for educators on integrating social and emotional learning into the curriculum, fostering positive behavior and leadership, and creating a culture of excellence in the classroom and school.

Collaborative for Academic, Social, and Emotional Learning (CASEL). casel.org. SEL program for whole schools or individual lessons.

National Alliance on Mental Illness (NAMI). nami.org. A thorough resource for support with mental illness at any age.

Positive Behavioral Interventions and Supports (PBIS). pbis.org. Whole-school behavior intervention program.

Books for Students

Coloring Book and Reflections for Social Emotional Learning by James Butler, M.Ed., illustrated by Becca Borrelli (Free Spirit, 2020). Reflect and relax with 36 calming, SEL-focused coloring activities for kids.

Dream Up Now: The Teen Journal for Creative Self-Discovery by Rayne Lacko, with community outreach advisor Lesley Holmes (Free Spirit, 2020). Teens explore emotions, create art, and envision life's possibilities with this guided, creative journal.

Feeling Worried! by Kay Barnham (Free Spirit, 2017). Help young children understand and cope with anxiety.

Man's Search for Meaning: Young Readers Edition by Viktor Frankl (Beacon Press, 2017). A nonfiction work for teen audiences describing the author's experiences in the concentration camps of Germany and his subsequent theories of counseling and human compassion.

Scaredy Squirrel by Mélanie Watt (Kids Can Press, 2008). My favorite children's picture book featuring an anxious scaredy squirrel.

Sea Prayer by Khaled Hosseini (Riverhead Books, 2018). A beautiful picture book for older children inspired by Syrian refugees missing home and seeking peace.

Seedfolks by Paul Fleischman, illustrated by Judy Pedersen (Harper Collins, 1997). A wonderful fiction book for grades 4 and up showing the power of community.

Simon vs. the Homo Sapiens Agenda by Becky Albertalli (Balzer + Bray, 2015). A novel for teen readers describing the feelings a young gay person may have as they grow into their self-advocacy and identity.

Sometimes When I'm Sad by Deborah Serani, Psy.D. (Free Spirit, 2020). A sensitive and supportive story to help young children recognize and cope with sadness.

Stamped: Racism, Antiracism, and You by Jason Reynolds and Ibram X. Kendi (Little Brown Books for Young Readers, 2020). An honest nonfiction book for young people on race and America that's perfect for reading groups.

Violet the Snowgirl by Lisa L. Walsh. (Free Spirit, 2020). This versatile story gives children permission to grieve and helps them find ways to cope with loss.

When a Friend Dies: A Book for Teens About Grieving & Healing by Marilyn E. Gootman, Ed.D. (Free Spirit, 2019). Sensitive advice and genuine understanding for teens coping with grief and loss.

INDEX

A

Action items, 4–5, 6
    At-A-Glance, 62–63
    for citywide trauma, 37–43, 63
    for mass-scale trauma, 48–54, 63
    for school-based trauma, 25–32, 62
    for self/home-based trauma, 10–19, 62
Activism, 32
Anti-bias resources, 31
Anti-racism, 24, 29, 41, 53

B

Black, Indigenous, and People of Color (BIPOC)
    citizens, 2, 26–27, 41

C

Calendar, crisis team, 28
Calling home, 11, 12–16, 31, 58, 62
CASEL, 53
Child Protective Services, 17, 41
Citywide trauma, 8, 35–44
    action items, 38, 63
    community maps, 38, 39–40
    community resources/contacts, 37–39
    digital communication, 42–44
    examples, 35
    impact, 36–37
    reaching out to community supports, 40–41
Classroom materials, 31
Coloring materials, 30
Community resource maps, 39–40, 63
Community resources/contacts, 30, 37–39,
    42–43, 63
Community supports, 40–41
Confidentiality, 24–25
Conversations with students and family
    members, 31
COVID-19 pandemic, 1
    adapting to, 45
    community resources, 38
    contact tracing, 21
    impact, 1–2, 7–8
    individualized interventions for students,
      46–47
    needs assessments, 18

Crisis kits. *See* Trauma kits
Crisis teams, 22–25, 26–29, 30, 62
Cultural centers, 41
Curriculum design/planning, 32–33, 49, 63

D

Data collection, 18–19
Digital learning/communication, 1, 15–16,
    42–44, 49–50, 51

E

Educator presence, 49–50
Emergency kit, of office supplies, 52–53
Emergency materials, 49, 63
Emergency numbers, 11, 17, 62

F

Families, building strong connections with,
    12–16
Family handouts, in trauma kit, 30
Financially struggling students, 26–27
Floyd, George, 2, 3, 35
Focus groups, 18–19

G

Gender-nonbinary students, 26
Global trauma. *See* State/country/world trauma
Gratitude journals/cards, 54
Guidebook, on trauma procedures, 16–18

H

Handouts, student/family, 30
Hurricanes, 39

I

Inclusive materials, 32
Inclusive school policy, 26–27
Information binder, 50, 52
Information, in trauma kit, 29, 30
Informed practices, 31–32
Institutional racism. *See* Systemic/institutional
    racism
Interventions
    data collection, 18–19
    tailoring for individual students, 46–49

J

Journals, 30, 54

L

LGBTQ students, 26–27
Listening to parents, 13

M

Manipulatives, in trauma kit, 30
Maps, community resource, 38, 39–40, 63
Mass-scale trauma. *See also* State/country/world
    trauma
    examples, 45
    layers of trauma, 8
Master information binder, 50, 52
Medical professionals, 41
Meditation practices, 49, 54, 59
Meetings, crisis team, 27, 28, 40
Mental well-being practices, 53–54
Military-connected students, 57
Mindfulness practices, 49, 51, 53–54, 59, 63

N

National Guard, 57
Needs assessments, 11, 18–19, 23, 62
Notebooks, in trauma kit, 30

O

Office supplies, 50, 52–53
Online learning. *See* Digital learning/
    communication

P

Pandemics. *See* COVID-19 pandemic
Protests, 36–37
Protocols, trauma response. *See* Trauma
    responses

Q

Questionnaires, needs assessment, 19

R

Racial slurs, 23
Racism, 23, 26, 29, 53. *See also* Systemic/
    institutional racism
Rapport building, 12
Relationship building, 11, 12–16, 62
Relationship violence, 23–24
Responsive Classroom, 53
Rethink SEL, 53
Retraumatization, 24, 25, 26–27, 31

S

School-based trauma, 4, 5, 21–32
    action items, 26, 62
    classroom materials and lesson planning,
        31–32
    crisis team, 22–29, 25, 26–29, 27
    curriculum planning, 31–32
    examples, 21
    layers of trauma, 8
    meetings, crisis team, 27–28
    trauma kit, 29–30
School closings, 1, 7–8
School counselors
    digital access to caseloads, 43–44
    expertise, 3
    goals, 3–4
    included in Trauma Response Guide, 17
    presence with students during mass-scale
        trauma, 49–50
    privacy issues, 24
    talking to parents, 13
    teachers communicating with, 10
Schoology, 42
School staff. *See also* School counselors; Teachers
    collective action by, 10
    communicating trauma procedures, 16–18
    crisis team, 22–25, 27
    each playing a part in trauma responses, 6, 10
    guidebook on trauma procedures for, 16–18
    informing others about personal lives of
        students, 24–25
Scripts for teachers, 14–16, 26, 29, 62
Second Step, 53
Self/home-based trauma, 4, 5
    action items, 10–11, 62
    building connections with families and
        students, 12–16
    examples, 7
    guidebook, trauma response, 16–18
    layers of trauma, 7–9
    needs assessments, 18–19
    recognizing signs, 9–10
SEL (social and emotional learning), 10, 48–49,
    51, 53, 63
September 11th terrorist attack, 46
Sexism, 24
Shootings, 36
Social and emotional learning (SEL). *See* SEL
    (social and emotional learning)

Social unrest, 36–37, 41
Socratic seminars, 32
Special needs students, 26–27
Staff. *See* School staff
State/country/world trauma, 4, 5, 45–54
   action items, 49, 63
   educator's presence, 49–50
   examples, 45
   individualized student intervention, 46–48
   preparing for a quick move, 50, 52–53
   schoolwide plans for in school and/or online
      learning, 50, 51
   SEL/mindfulness practices, 53–54
   shared experiences/emotions, 45–46
Statement blueprints, 26, 60, 62
Stress
   practices for coping with, 53–54
   signs of, in students, 9–10, 58
   on students during school closings, 7–8
Student development, trauma and, 4
Student handouts, 30
Students. *See also* Self/home-based trauma
   building relationships, 11, 12–16
   contact information, 38, 63
   conversations, 31
   COVID-19, 2, 7, 8–9
   establishing presence, 49, 63
   impact of school closings on, 7–8
   inclusive school policy and, 26–27
   needs assessments, 18–19
   retraumatization, 25–26
   sharing community resources, 42–43
   sources of trauma, 4, 5
   supporting military-connected, 57
Student voice projects, 54
Symbolism, evaluating, 32
Systemic/institutional racism, 2, 9, 26, 29, 41, 53

T

Teachers. *See also* School staff
   communicating with school counseling
      office, 10
   crisis team, 22, 28

digital presence with students, 50, 51
emergency kit, 52–53
master information binder, 50, 52
Quick Sheet for Trauma Responses, 58–59
scripts for, 14–16, 26, 29, 62
student privacy issues, 24–25
using digital page on student caseloads,
   43–44
Translation services, 41
Trauma kits, 26, 29–30, 39, 59, 62
Trauma procedures, in trauma kit, 30
Trauma Response Preparations Worksheet for
   School Planning, 60–61
Trauma response protocol, 27
Trauma responses
   for citywide trauma, 37–44
   communicating procedures to staff members,
      16–18
   establishing a schoolwide, 11
   for mass-scale trauma, 48–54
   Preparations Worksheet for School Planning,
      60–61
   purpose, 4
   questions related to, 5
   for school-based trauma, 25–32
   school staff contributions, 6
   for self/home-based trauma, 10–19
   Teacher Quick Sheet, 58–59

U

Urban League, 41

W

Wi-Fi accessibility, 42
Wi-Fi providers, 41

Z

Zoom, 1

Digital versions of all reproducible forms can be downloaded at
freespirit.com/trauma. Use the password **2respond**.

ABOUT THE AUTHOR

Stephanie Filio is a middle school counselor for Virginia Beach City Public Schools. As a young mom, she was empowered by her high school counselor to continue pursuing her dreams, and she received her undergraduate degree in interdisciplinary studies from the University of Virginia and her M.Ed. in counseling from Old Dominion University. In a discussion with one of her UVA professors about her desire to stay in school forever, her mentor responded, "If you want to be a lifelong learner, go into education," and  so she found her place. Prior to her eight years as a public school counselor, Stephanie worked in private education, specializing in standardized tests, test preparation, and future planning. She writes about SEL and educational topics for the Free Spirit Publishing Blog and about her career and hobbies at her blog Weekend Therapy (weekendtherapy.wordpress.com), and she can be found on Twitter @steffschoolcoun. Stephanie also enjoys spending time with her books, crafts, and family.

Other Great Resources from Free Spirit

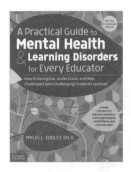

A Practical Guide to Mental Health & Learning Disorders for Every Educator
How to Recognize, Understand, and Help Challenged (and Challenging) Students Succeed (Revised & Updated Edition)
by Myles L. Cooley, Ph.D.

For educators and counselors, grades K–12.
256 pp.; PB; 8½" x 11"; includes digital content.

Teach for Attention!
A Tool Belt of Strategies for Engaging Students with Attention Challenges
by Ezra Werb, M.Ed.

For educators, grades K–8.
208 pp.; PB; 6" x 7½".

Boost Emotional Intelligence in Students
30 Flexible Researched-Based Activities to Build EQ Skills (Grades 5–9)
by Maurice J. Elias, Ph.D., and Steven E. Tobias, Psy.D.

For teachers and counselors, grades 5–9.
192 pp.; PB; 8½" x 11"; includes digital content.

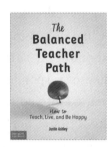

The Balanced Teacher Path
How to Teach, Live, and Be Happy
by Justin Ashley

For educators, grades K–8.
160 pp.; PB; 7¼" x 9¼".

Inspiring Student Empowerment
Moving Beyond Engagement, Refining Differentiation
by Patti Drapeau

For educators, grades K–12.
208 pp.; PB; 8½" x 11"; includes digital content.

Free PLC/Book Study Guide
freespirit.com/PLC

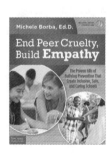

End Peer Cruelty, Build Empathy
The Proven 6Rs of Bullying Prevention That Create Inclusive, Safe, and Caring Schools
by Michele Borba, Ed.D.

For administrators, teachers, counselors, youth leaders, bullying prevention teams, and parents of children in grades K–8.
288 pp; PB; 7¼" x 9¼"; includes digital content.

Free PLC/Book Study Guide
freespirit.com/PLC

Interested in purchasing multiple quantities and receiving volume discounts?
Contact edsales@freespirit.com or call 1.800.735.7323 and ask for Education Sales.

Many Free Spirit authors are available for speaking engagements, workshops, and keynotes.
Contact speakers@freespirit.com or call 1.800.735.7323.

For pricing information, to place an order, or to request a free catalog, contact:

Free Spirit Publishing Inc. • 6325 Sandburg Road, Suite 100 • Minneapolis, MN 55427-3674
toll-free 800.735.7323 • local 612.338.2068 • fax 612.337.5050
help4kids@freespirit.com • freespirit.com